Caribbean Primary Science

Level 3

Contributors

Karen Morrison

Susan Crumpton

Lorraine DeAllie

Lisa Greenstein

Sally Knowlman

HODDER
EDUCATION
AN HACHETTE UK COMPANY

Hachette UK's policy is to use papers that are natural, renewable and recyclable products and made from wood grown in well-managed forests and other controlled sources. The logging and manufacturing processes are expected to conform to the environmental regulations of the country of origin.

Orders: please contact Bookpoint Ltd, 130 Park Drive, Milton Park, Abingdon, Oxon OX14 4SE. Telephone: +44 (0)1235 827827. Fax: +44 (0)1235 400401. Email education@bookpoint.co.uk
Lines are open from 9 a.m. to 5 p.m., Monday to Saturday, with a 24-hour message answering service. You can also order through our website: www.hoddereducation.com

ISBN: 978 1 5104 7894 7

© Cloud Publishing Services, Susan Crumpton, Lorraine DeAllie, Lisa Greenstein, Sally Knowlman 2020

First published in 2020 by
Hodder Education,
An Hachette UK Company
Carmelite House
50 Victoria Embankment
London EC4Y 0DZ
www.hoddereducation.com

Impression number   10 9 8 7 6 5 4 3 2 1

Year   2023 2022 2021 2020

Main cover illustration by Heather Clarke/D'Avila Illustration, Seahorse design by Andrew Painter/ D'Avila Illustration
Illustrations by Leo Daly and Magriet Brink, Creative House; Heidel Dedekind; Claudia Eckard; Jiggs Snaddon Wood
Typeset in FS Albert by Jenny Wheeldon
Printed in Slovenia

A catalogue record for this title is available from the British Library.

MIX
Paper from
responsible sources
FSC™ C104740
www.fsc.org

The Publishers would like to thank the following for permission to reproduce copyright material.

Photo credits

www.stock.adobe.com: p.3 (tl) © New Africa/stock.adobe.com, (tr) © 1L26/stock.adobe.com, (mr/bm) & p.7 (m) © writerfantast/stock.adobe.com, (bl) © evgenica/stock.adobe.com, (br) © sarawuth123/stock. adobe.com; p.7 (t) & p.30 (bl) © corund/stock.adobe.com, (b) & p.41 (br) © Yong Hian Lim/stock.adobe.com; p.8 (t) © karenfoleyphoto/stock.adobe.com, (b) © Robert/stock.adobe.com; p.9 (t) © Gene/stock.adobe.com, (b) © Tomas Ragina/stock.adobe.com; p.10 © willyam/stock.adobe.com; p.14 (tr) © johnmerlin/stock.adobe. com; p.16 (l) © Passakorn/stock.adobe.com, (r) © Africa Studio/stock.adobe.com; p.17 (tl) © Jane Kelly/stock. adobe.com, (tm) © juliars/stock.adobe.com, (tr) © nadyac/stock.adobe.com, (b) © tonktiti/stock.adobe.com; p.20 (tl) © rosendo/stock.adobe.com, (tm) © DigitalGenetics/stock.adobe.com, (tr) © Fireworks Pixels/stock. adobe.com, (bl) © Khvost/stock.adobe.com, (bm) © ImagePixel/stock.adobe.com, (br) © Ruslan Kudrin/ stock.adobe.com; p.26 (t) © W.Scott McGill/stock.adobe.com, (m) © Simon Dannhauer/stock.adobe.com, (b) © Stephen Bonk/stock.adobe.com; p.27 (t) © TK6/stock.adobe.com, (b) © 5second/stock.adobe.com; p.29 (tl) © Nicolas VINCENT/stock.adobe.com, (tm) © Tshi/stock.adobe.com, (tr) © Conrad/stock.adobe.com, (bl) © Rafa Irusta/stock.adobe.com, (2bl) © alinamd/stock.adobe.com, (2br) © Georg Lehnerer/stock.adobe. com, (br) © ValentinValkov/stock.adobe.com; p.30 (tl) © Ekkarin/stock.adobe.com, (2tl) © DiamondGalaxy/ stock.adobe.com, (2tr) © atoss/stock.adobe.com, (tr) © jStock/stock.adobe.com, (ml) © Pilipipa/stock.adobe. com, (m) © WDnet Studio/stock.adobe.com, (mr) © makistock/stock.adobe.com, (bm) © Dzha/stock.adobe. com, (br) © VAKSMANV/stock.adobe.com; p.31 (tl) © Aleksandr Matveev/stock.adobe.com, (tm) © Roger/ stock.adobe.com, (tr) © bilanol/stock.adobe.com, (ml) © Sebastian/stock.adobe.com, (m) © Glass Hat Digital/stock.adobe.com, (mr) © savelov/stock.adobe.com, (bl) © Andreas/stock.adobe.com, (bm) © bennyartist/stock.adobe.com, (br) © Nik_Merkulov/stock.adobe.com; p.33 (t) © photka/stock.adobe.com, (m) © Olga Galushko/stock.adobe.com, (b) © Bohdan/stock.adobe.com; p.38 (l) © grafikplusfoto/stock. adobe.com, (m) © ALF photo/stock.adobe.com, (r) © Nina/stock.adobe.com; p.40 (tl) © Sergejs/stock.adobe. com, (tr) © photopixel/stock.adobe.com, (ml) © toa555/stock.adobe.com, (mr) © Nevada31/stock.adobe. com, (bl) © Kalyakan/stock.adobe.com, (br) © Rawpixel.com/stock.adobe.com; p.41 (tl) © brgfx/stock.adobe. com, (ml) © Sonate/stock.adobe.com, (2ml) © maxcity/stock.adobe.com, (2mr) © fancytapis/stock.adobe. com, (mr) © todja/stock.adobe.com, (bl) © ksena32/stock.adobe.com, (2bl) © dule964/stock.adobe.com, (2br) © Ruslan Ivantsov/stock.adobe.com; p.42 © Prostock-studio/stock.adobe.com; p.43 (tl) © kiboka/stock. adobe.com, (2tl) © dule964/stock.adobe.com, (2tr) © zevana/stock.adobe.com, (tr) © Hyrma/stock.adobe. com, (bl) © Pixel-Shot/stock.adobe.com, (2bl) © Andreas/stock.adobe.com, (2br) © Tatiana Gasich/stock. adobe.com, (br) © samuelgarces/stock.adobe.com; p.44 © Vadimsadovski/stock.adobe.com; p.45 © Revenant/ stock.adobe.com; p.46/47 © klyaksun/stock.adobe.com; p.48 (tl) © brutto film/stock.adobe.com, (tr) © 1xpert/ stock.adobe.com, (ml) © Artsiom Petrushenka/stock.adobe.com, (mr) © Matthieu/stock.adobe.com, (bl) © robert/stock.adobe.com, (br) © alinamd/stock.adobe.com; p.50 (t) © Richard Griffin/stock.adobe.com; p.53 (l) © pamela_d_mcadams/stock.adobe.com, (r) © ekyaky/stock.adobe.com; p.54 (tl) © eqroy/stock.adobe. com, (tm) © Laurrie Basiletti/stock.adobe.com, (tr) © iamtk/stock.adobe.com, (bl) © jkraft5/stock.adobe. com, (bm) © Topfotolia/stock.adobe.com, (br) © Jacquelin/stock.adobe.com; p.55 (tl) © meepoohyaphoto/stock. adobe.com, (tr) © Lena Bukovsky/stock.adobe.com; p.56 (bl) © ammina/stock.adobe.com, (2bl) © マルヤマゴーヘイ/ stock.adobe.com, (bm & br) © lightgirl/stock.adobe.com, (2br) © kolesnikovserg/stock.adobe.com; p.57 (tl) © psartstudio/stock.adobe.com, (2tl) © tada/stock.adobe.com, (2tr) © Kazakova Maryia/stock. adobe.com, (tr) © juliars/stock.adobe.com; p.61 (tl) © pannipa/stock.adobe.com, (b) © Oliver/stock.adobe.com; p.62 (t) © Mushy/stock.adobe.com, (m) © Kazakova Maryia/stock.adobe.com; p.64 (l) © ann_minsk/stock. adobe.com, (m) © Gulsina/stock.adobe.com; p.67 © PIXbank/stock.adobe.com; p.72 © gerasimov174/ stock.adobe.com; p.73 © Richard Carey/stock.adobe.com; p.78 (t) & 137 (bm) © Catmando/stock.adobe.com, (b) © v_paulava/stock.adobe.com; p.81 © Oscar/stock.adobe.com; p.82 (tl) © Janet Muir/Danita Delimont/ stock.adobe.com, (tm) © mzphoto11/stock.adobe.com, (tr) © Uryadnikov Sergey/stock.adobe.com; p.83 (tl) © creativenature.nl/stock.adobe.com, (2tl) © Joe/stock.adobe.com, (2tr) © Dmitry Rukhlenko/stock.adobe. com, (tr) © emranashraf/stock.adobe.com, (ml) © Stef Bennett/stock.adobe.com, (2ml) © ondrejprosicky/stock. adobe.com, (2mr) © Roman Stetsyk/stock.adobe.com, (mr) © ipekmorel/stock.adobe.com, (bl) © Lea/stock. adobe.com, (bm) © Chelsea/stock.adobe.com, (br) © Joel Toryd/stock.adobe.com; p.84 (tl) © ffolas/stock. adobe.com, (2tl) © Gcapture/stock.adobe.com, (2tr) © valkoinen7/stock.adobe.com, (tr) © thongsan/stock. adobe.com, (bl) © modustollens/stock.adobe.com, (bm) © monticellllo/stock.adobe.com, (br) © ffolas/stock. adobe.com; p.87 (t) © YesPhotographers/stock.adobe.com; p.89 (tl) © bullet_chained/stock.adobe.com, (tr) & p.154 (tr) © blueringmedia/stock.adobe.com, (mr) & p.154 (br) © wectorcolor/stock.adobe.com, (m) & p.154 (rm) © zolotons/stock.adobe.com, (ml) & p.154 (tl) © FARBAI/stock.adobe.com, (bl) & p.154 (bl) © Kazakova Maryia/stock.adobe.com, (br) © leopride/stock.adobe.com; p.93 (tl) © chaiyon021/stock.adobe. com, (tr) © Hamilton/stock.adobe.com; p.96 © wirojsid/stock.adobe.com; p.110 (t) © GingerCat/stock.adobe. com, (b) © Nurlan/stock.adobe.com; p.111 (t) © Kazakova Maryia/stock.adobe.com; p.112 (b) © Alexandr Vasilyev/stock.adobe.com, (br) © ALEXEI/stock.adobe.com; p.114 (bl) & p.117 (b) © Manuel Soler/stock.adobe. com, (br) © diy13/stock.adobe.com; p.116 (tl) © realstock1/stock.adobe.com, (tm) © brizmaker/stock.adobe. com, (tr) © Геннадий Кулиненко/Gennady Kulinenko/stock.adobe.com, (ml) © gerasimenuk/stock.adobe. com, (m) © Scanrail/stock.adobe.com, (mr) © Shawn Hempel/stock.adobe.com, (b) © hvostik16/stock.adobe. com; p.118 (bl) © Alex/stock.adobe.com, (bm) © Lukas Gojda/stock.adobe.com, (br) © Pongvit/stock.adobe. com, (br); p.119 © Семен Саливанчук/stock.adobe.com; p.128 © Victor/stock.adobe.com; p.136 (tl) © Cheryl Davis/stock.adobe.com, (tr) © darekb22/stock.adobe.com, (br) © vadim yerofeyev/stock.adobe.com; p.137 (t) © Alik Mulikov/stock.adobe.com, (mtl) © kovaleva_ka/stock.adobe.com, (mtr) © MIGUEL GARCIA SAAVED/ stock.adobe.com, (mbl) © aleksandarfilip/stock.adobe.com, (mbm) © Eric Isselée/stock.adobe.com, (mbr) © lewal2010/stock.adobe.com, (bl) © frantisek hojdysz/stock.adobe.com, (br) © MarcoBagnoli Elflaco/stock. adobe.com; p.138 © NancieLee/stock.adobe.com; p.139 (t) © Papa Bravo/stock.adobe.com, (b) © Evita/stock. adobe.com; p.140 (t) © New Africa/stock.adobe.com, (b) © Kirill Zdorov/stock.adobe.com; p.141 © natashaphoto/ stock.adobe.com; p.144 (t) © heinteh/stock.adobe.com, (b) © Sashkin/stock.adobe.com; p.145 (t) © Nigel/ stock.adobe.com, (b) © cecile02/stock.adobe.com; p.146 © Wutthikrai/stock.adobe.com; p.148 (t) © designua/stock.adobe.com, (bl) © 孤飞的鹤/stock.adobe.com, (bm) © kelifamily/stock.adobe.com, (br) © Karlis/ stock.adobe.com; p.149 (t) © Sasajo/stock.adobe.com; p.154 (ml) © adogslifephoto/stock.adobe.com; p.156 © Alisa/stock.adobe.com. **Alamy.com:** p.107 (t) © Max McClure/AlamyStockPhoto.com; **Mike van der Wolk (+27 83 268 6000; mike@springhigh.co.za):** [all © Mike van der Wolk] p.50 (b); p.51 (both); p.67 (m); p.87 (b); p.100 (all); p.121 (b); p.124 (b); p.125 (b); p.130; p.131 (t); p.132 (b); p.134; p.142; p.144 (b); p.147; p.149 (b); **Shutterstock.com:** (ml) p.3 © Studio BM/Shutterstock.com; p.60 © Yanawut Suntornkij/Shutterstock.com; p.72 (b) © Christophe Rouziou/Shutterstock.com; p.93 (b) © ElinaKS/Shutterstock.com; p.102 © Pawel Kazmierczak/Shutterstock.com; p.107 (b) © Gabriela Beres/Shutterstock.com; p.118 (t) © Isles of Sand/ Shutterstock.com; p.124 (t) © Erickson Stock/Shutterstock.com

Contents

How to use this book

This Student's Book covers the key strands and requirements outlined in the OECS Primary Grades' Standards for Science and Technology in a way that allows teachers to cover their regional curricula thoroughly and efficiently. The student material provides both learning notes and a range of activities to help and encourage students to fully meet the standards for the level.

There are ten topics in the book. Topic 1: **Being a scientist** explicitly covers key skills that students will revisit and use as they work through the course. Topics 2–10 correspond with the science strands **Earth and Space** (Topics 2, 3 and 4); **Life Science** (Topics 5, 6 and 7) and **Physical Science** (Topics 8, 9 and 10). Each topic is divided into sub-strands with a number of units that cover the required content and skills. Teachers can work through the book as it is, or choose topics to match their planning.

Each of Topics 2–10 has an opening section with the following features:

Notes for teachers which highlight prior knowledge and give information about content and skills covered in the topic.

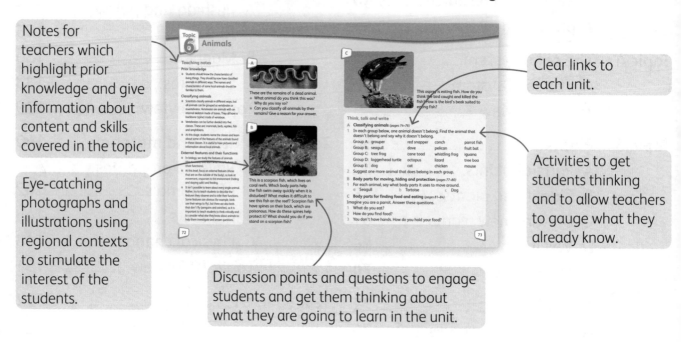

Clear links to each unit.

Activities to get students thinking and to allow teachers to gauge what they already know.

Eye-catching photographs and illustrations using regional contexts to stimulate the interest of the students.

Discussion points and questions to engage students and get them thinking about what they are going to learn in the unit.

The questions and photographs relate to the specific units in each topic. You can let the students do all of the activities (A, B, C and D, for example) as you start a topic, or you can focus on the activities that relate to the unit you will be teaching.

Brief teaching notes are provided at the start of each topic. These tell you what you can expect from students and give some details about the content of each unit.

The units are structured in a similar, easy-to-follow, way.

The unit opener pages contain:

Information boxes which explain concepts and provide examples.

A student-friendly list of learning objectives

A list of key words for the unit. These words are blue in the text.

The student materials contain a range of different types of activities with the main skills used in the activity highlighted.

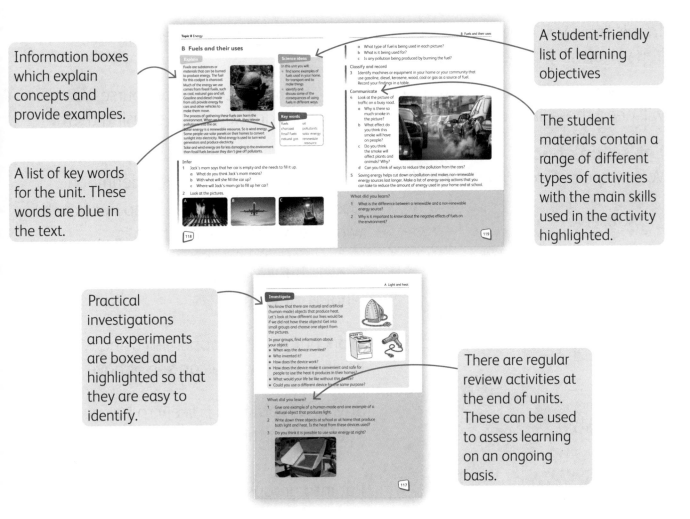

Practical investigations and experiments are boxed and highlighted so that they are easy to identify.

There are regular review activities at the end of units. These can be used to assess learning on an ongoing basis.

As you work through the topics, you will find a wide range of different types of activities and tasks, including practical investigations, experiments and research-based tasks. These features are all clearly marked so that you can easily find them.

The topics end with a review section that provides:

* A summary activity that actively involves students and helps them develop summarising skills at the same time as consolidating what they have learnt.

* Think, talk and write activities which encourage students to share ideas, clarify their thinking and develop healthy and critical attitudes to science and technology.

* A quick check set of revision questions drawn from different units in the topic. These can be used for consolidation or as short tests at the end of the topic.

Topic 1 — Being a scientist

In this topic you are going to learn more about the skills that scientists use. You will also try these skills out yourself.

Last year you used some skills as you worked through your science course. You will need these skills again this year, and you will learn new ways of using them.

Let's think back

Work in pairs. Take turns to match each skill on the left to its correct definition.

Observe	Use special instruments to find out how long, wide, heavy or hot something is.
Measure	Look carefully to find what is the same and what is different.
Record	Work out what is happening using what you know and what you can see or have read.
Classify	Say what you think is likely to happen before you do something.
Infer	Put into groups using different features.
Predict	Read information from tables and graphs and work out what it tells you.
Experiment	Write down or draw what you find out.
Design	Plan and choose materials to build or make something.
Interpret data	Do a test to see what happens.

Let's measure scientifically

We use different measuring instruments and units of measurement to investigate objects and conditions in science.

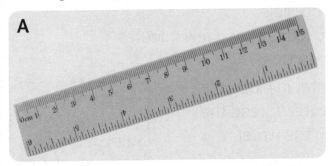

A

We use a ruler to measure length and height. We can measure in different units, for example, metres, centimetres and millimetres.

B

We measure how heavy things are using a balance scale. Heavy objects are measured in kilograms, and lighter objects are measured in grams.

C

We can measure how much liquid we have by using a measuring jug and looking carefully at the marked units. This jug shows litres and millilitres.

D

A thermometer measures temperature and tells us how hot or cold it is. Temperature is measured in degrees. You can use degrees Celsius or degrees Fahrenheit.

Read the measurement each picture shows. Write each measurement in your book with the correct units.

A

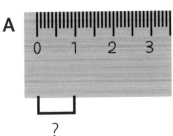

?

B

C

Let's use a thermometer

When we measure temperature, it is important to get an accurate measurement. There are some simple steps you can take to make sure your measurements are as accurate as possible.

* Set up your equipment or experiment and leave it for a few minutes before you measure and record any temperatures.

* Read the measurement on the thermometer in place. For example, if you are measuring how hot water is, read the measurement while the thermometer is in the water.

* Shake the thermometer gently to reset the liquid or let it return to room temperature before using it for a different task.

> **Safety note**
> Always be careful when you are using a thermometer, as it can break easily.

1   Record the temperature shown on each of these thermometers.

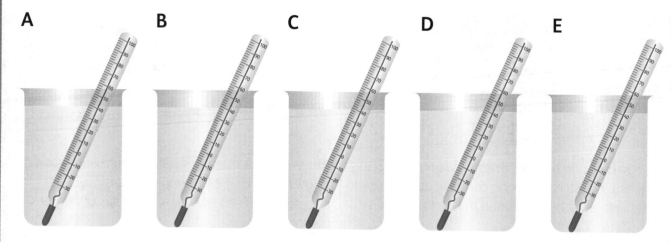

A   B   C   D   E

2   Which liquid is closest to freezing? Explain how you know this.

3   Use a thermometer to measure and record the temperature:
   a   of tap water
   b   of cold water (from the fridge)
   c   inside your classroom
   d   outside in the Sun
   e   outside in the shade.

Let's do experiments and fair tests

We do experiments to find the answers to questions. For example, what happens to candy if we put it into hot, cool and cold water?

To answer the question, you need to plan what you will do and work out what equipment you will use. You should also think about safety.

For example, I will get three candies and put them into water from the kettle, water from the tap and water from the fridge. I will need three candies, three containers for water and hot, cool and cold water.

I will need to be careful with the hot water, as it can burn.

When you do an experiment or scientific investigation, you need to make sure that you are doing a fair test.

When you do a fair test, you change one thing only. You keep all the other things in the experiment the same.

1   How does changing only one thing make a test fair? Discuss this in your groups.

2   Look at this experiment that Ambika has set up.

Cup A   Cup B   Cup C

Hot water   Cold water   Ice-cold water

Answer these questions about the experiment.
a   What did Ambika change?
b   What three things did she keep the same?
c   How did Ambika make sure she was doing a fair test?
d   Predict what you think her results will be. Give a reason for your answer.

Let's ask questions

You can do an investigation to find the answers to scientific questions.

Some questions can be answered by doing a fair test. Some questions need to be answered in other ways.

Read these questions.

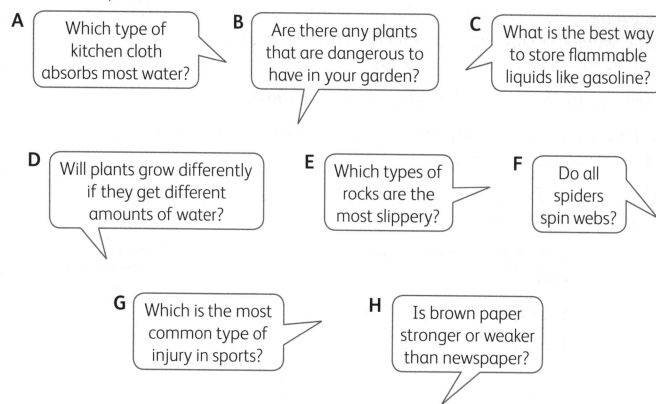

A Which type of kitchen cloth absorbs most water?

B Are there any plants that are dangerous to have in your garden?

C What is the best way to store flammable liquids like gasoline?

D Will plants grow differently if they get different amounts of water?

E Which types of rocks are the most slippery?

F Do all spiders spin webs?

G Which is the most common type of injury in sports?

H Is brown paper stronger or weaker than newspaper?

1 Make a table like this one in your book.

These questions can be answered by doing a fair test	These questions cannot be answered by doing a fair test

2 Sort the questions into two groups and write the letters in the correct columns in your table.

3 Look at the questions that cannot be answered by doing a fair test. Discuss in groups how you could answer these.

Let's answer questions

Here are some methods that scientists use to answer questions when they cannot do a fair test.

* Observe and compare: When you look closely or watch something you are observing it. We compare things by looking at how they are similar and how they are different.

* Measure and record: Scientists take measurements over time to find out how things change or grow, they may repeat their measurements to make sure they are accurate. It is important to record both the measurements and the units of measurement.

* Carry out a survey: When you do a survey you collect and record data to answer your question. Some surveys involve interviewing people to get their responses, others involve counting or comparing objects.

* Using sources: You may need to look for information in books or on the internet to answer some questions. You can also ask experts to find the answer to your questions.

Which method would you use to find the answers to these questions about paper?

1   How is paper made?

2   How many people in your community recycle used paper?

3   What happens to newspaper if you bury it in the soil?

4   Do different kinds of paper all cost the same?

5   What craft items are made from paper?

6   Draw a table like this one in your book. Fill in two examples of science questions you could answer using each method.

Observe and compare	Measure and record	Do a survey	Use sources

Teaching notes

Prior knowledge

✱ Students observed different types of weather in Level 2, and they also used different instruments to measure and predict weather. They designed and made wind vanes. Many of the key words should be familiar. Remind students of the different states of matter (solid, liquid, gas), and relate these to water in its different states (ice, liquid water, water vapour). They should also be familiar with the basic water cycle.

Elements of weather

✱ The elements of weather are air/wind, clouds, water vapour, precipitation and temperature. Make it a regular practice to ask students about the day's weather conditions. Draw their attention to each element. They should observe details outside the classroom.

Wind

✱ If possible, have a real anemometer to show the students. If that is not possible, print out pictures of anemometers. Collect the materials required for the anemometer design project so that these are ready for the lesson.

The water cycle

✱ Repeat and reinforce water cycle vocabulary to ensure that students can distinguish clearly between the main terms: evaporation, condensation, precipitation. It is useful to link the terms to related words (evaporate – vapour – evaporation; condensation – condense). Students should understand that the Sun is the main heat source that powers the water cycle.

Temperature

✱ Students will need to measure temperature using thermometers. Bring a thermometer to class for this unit.

Can John's stone really predict the weather?

What makes the sign funny?

Where do clouds come from?

How do they form?

Where do they go when they disappear?

C

How does water move between the atmosphere and the Earth's surface?
How does the water cycle work?

D

How hot does it get where you live?
How do you measure how hot it is?

Think, talk and write

A Elements of weather
(pages 10–11)

Do you remember the main elements of weather? Work in pairs. List the five elements of weather.

B Wind *(pages 12–15)*

In pairs or groups, brainstorm all the words you can use to describe clouds and wind. Write your ideas on a large sheet of paper.

C The water cycle *(pages 16–19)*

Draw a simple diagram of the water cycle to show what you remember from last year.

D Temperature *(pages 20–24)*

Sofia says: 'Yesterday the temperature was 23 °C. Today it's 39 °C and tomorrow it will be 40 °C! But next week will be cool again.'

1 What is happening to the temperature?

2 Which temperature sounds most uncomfortable? Why?

3 Which sounds most unlikely for next week: 5 °C, 15 °C, 22 °C? Explain your answer.

A Elements of weather

The **atmosphere** is a layer of **air** over the Earth's surface. When we talk about the weather, we talk about the conditions of the atmosphere at a particular place and time. There are five main **elements** of weather:

* **Wind** is moving air.
* **Water vapour** is the evaporated water in the atmosphere.
* **Clouds** form when the water **vapour** condenses and tiny water droplets gather in the sky.
* **Precipitation** is the water that forms in the atmosphere or on the Earth's surface. In the Caribbean, precipitation is usually dew or rain.
* Air **temperature** tells us how warm or cool the air is. Heat from the Sun warms up the Earth's surface.

When we talk about the weather, we usually talk about all five of its elements.

Science ideas

In this unit you will:
* explain what weather is
* identify and name the elements of weather.

Key words

atmosphere	clouds
air	vapour
elements	precipitation
wind	temperature
water vapour	

Classify

1   Copy and complete this paragraph about the weather today.

The weather today is _____.
I feel _____. I can see _____
clouds in the sky. I think the weather tomorrow will be _____
because _____.

2   What is your favourite kind of weather? What is your least favourite kind of weather? Draw and label a picture showing your favourite and least favourite kinds of weather. Show each of the five elements of weather in each picture.

Did you know that rainbows occur because of tiny water droplets in the air around us?

Observe and infer

3 Describe the weather in each picture and note any similarities and differences.

What did you learn?

1 Unscramble the names of the five elements of weather.

   a pteeraturem   **b** aewtr ovupra   **c** onatppiticire

   d uodscl   **e** nidw

2 For each activity, write down the weather conditions that do **not** match.

a

   hiking   sunny, clear skies   light clouds   dark, heavy clouds

b

   flying a kite   no wind   light breeze   very strong wind

c

   swimming   no wind   light clouds   thunder clouds

B Wind

Science ideas

In this unit you will:

* explain the useful and harmful effects of wind
* design, make and use an anemometer.

Explain

Wind is air that moves in the Earth's atmosphere. **Wind energy** can push and pull things. This can be very useful, for example, when it powers sailboats and windmills. Very strong winds can have harmful effects. Wind can damage buildings and other structures.

When the wind wears away soil and rocks, this is called wind **erosion**. **Wind speed** is a measure of how fast the wind is blowing. We measure wind speed using an **anemometer**.

Key words

wind energy
erosion   .
wind speed
anemometer

Observe and compare

1   Match each picture to a suitable label.

A

B

C

(blow seeds)   (dry laundry)   (provide power for sailboats)

(blow over trees and plants)   (help aeroplanes move faster)

(turn windmills to generate electricity)

cause erosion of rocks and land

tear down buildings and other structures

move sand and soil to create beaches and dunes

2 Say whether each picture shows a useful or harmful effect of wind.
Give a reason.

13

Design and make

An anemometer is an instrument that measures wind speed. It has cups that catch the wind, and it measures how fast they turn. In this activity you will construct an anemometer.

You will need: a single-hole punch, 2 plastic straws, 5 small paper cups, a pushpin, a pencil with an eraser on the end.

Your teacher will provide a fan and a stopwatch to test your anemometers.

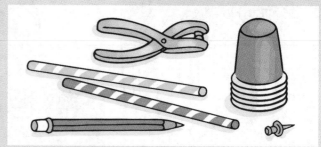

Step 1:

Use the hole punch to punch four holes, opposite each other, just under the rim of one cup. Push the two straws through the holes.

Step 2:

In the four remaining cups, punch two holes about 4 cm apart, halfway down the cup. Use each of the four straw ends to attach a cup. The cups must all face the same direction.

Step 3:

Use the sharpened pencil to poke a hole through the bottom of the middle cup. Then push the pencil, eraser first, through the hole. Wiggle it so the hole isn't tight. Gently push the pushpin through the straws into the pencil eraser. Don't push it too far, as it needs to spin.

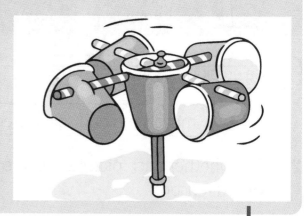

Step 4:

Gently push the cups to make them spin around.

If the structure is too tight to spin, try loosening the pencil or the pin.

Step 5:

Mark one of the cups so that you can see how often it goes around.

Evaluate your design

To use your anemometer, you need a fan with slow, medium and fast settings, and a timer or stopwatch.

1   Place the anemometer in front of the fan. Let someone count how many times the cups go round.

2   Record your observations in a table like this one:

Fan setting	1	2	3
Number of times the cups rotated in 30 seconds			

3   How would a real anemometer differ from your model?

What did you learn?

1   List three useful and three harmful effects of wind.

2   In your own words, explain for what we use wind anemometers.

C The water cycle

Explain

Surface water is the water on the Earth's surface, for example, in rivers, lakes, oceans and streams. There is also water under the ground, called **ground water**. Heat from the Sun causes surface water to **evaporate** and turn to **water vapour**. Water vapour rises into the atmosphere. As it rises, it cools and turns back to liquid droplets. This is called **condensation**. The tiny water droplets gather to form **clouds**. Eventually, the droplets join and get heavier. They fall back to Earth as rain. The constant movement of water between the Earth's surface and the atmosphere is known as the water cycle.

Science ideas

In this unit you will:
* observe the evaporation and condensation of water
* describe and demonstrate how clouds form
* identify the heat source that powers the water cycle
* explain the process of the water cycle.

Observe

Key words

surface water
ground water
evaporate
water vapour
condensation
clouds

1   Carry out an experiment to observe condensation.
    You will need: cups, juice or soda, ice cubes, a paper napkin.

    a   Make sure the cups are dry.

    b   Pour the drinks into the cups and add ice.

    c   Observe what happens on the outside of the cup.

    d   Pat the outside of the cup gently with the paper napkin. What do you observe?

    e   What do you think caused this to happen?

    f   Jake says: 'The droplets come from inside the cups.' Why is Jake wrong?

    g   Which is the correct name for the process you observed: evaporation or condensation? Give a reason for your answer.

Experiment

1 Look at these three experiments to observe evaporation.

A

water —
stove —
pot

B

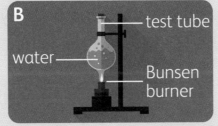

test tube
water —
Bunsen burner

C

Sun
water —
basin —

a Only one of these three experiments is safe to leave unattended. Which one is it? Give a reason for your answer.

b Identify the heat source in each experiment.

c Choose one experiment. Make notes about your experiment using these headings:
  * Aim (what you are trying to find out)
  * Hypothesis (predict what you think will happen)
  * Steps
  * Safety procedures
  * Observations (what actually happened)
  * Conclusion (what the experiment showed)

Research

2 How do clouds form?

Share your ideas in groups.

Do some research to find out what makes clouds form.

Communicate

3   Work in groups. Use the information on this page to help you create a song or rap that explains the water cycle. Make sure to:

  ✳ identify the heat source that powers the water cycle

  ✳ explain evaporation and condensation

  ✳ include the words rain, clouds and surface water.

Clouds

Cool c

Precipitation
Rain

Condensation
Water vapour cools
and changes back
to water droplets.

Runoff
Water that flows over the
Earth's surface towards the sea

Ground water
Water that lies in the soil
and deep underground

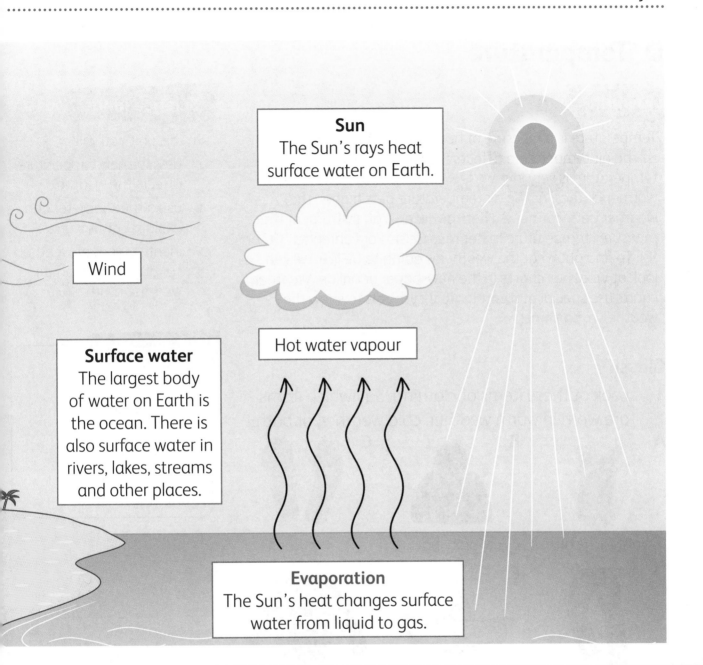

Sun
The Sun's rays heat surface water on Earth.

Wind

Hot water vapour

Surface water
The largest body of water on Earth is the ocean. There is also surface water in rivers, lakes, streams and other places.

Evaporation
The Sun's heat changes surface water from liquid to gas.

What did you learn?

1   Write two sentences to explain the difference between evaporation and condensation.

2   Imagine that you're trying to explain to a younger child how clouds form. How could you demonstrate the process?

3   Zak says: 'If there were no Sun, we could just use electricity to power the water cycle.' Explain Zak's mistake.

D Temperature

Explain

Temperature is a measure of how hot or cold something is. The air temperature **affects** the weather. When the air temperature is very low, we feel cold. We may need to wear warmer clothes. As the air temperature gets higher, the weather gets warmer. A **thermometer** is an instrument that measures temperature in **degrees** Celsius or Fahrenheit (°C or °F). To find out what the weather is going to be like, we can look at **weather charts** in the newspaper or online. Weather charts use special **meteorological symbols** to show the weather **conditions**.

Science ideas

In this unit you will:
* describe how temperature affects the weather
* use a thermometer and explain how it works
* identify types of weather conditions by examining weather charts.

Key words

affect
thermometer
degrees
weather charts
meteorological symbol
conditions

Classify

1 Look at these items of clothing. Say which items are worn in warm weather, cold weather, or both.

A

bathing suit

B

woolly hat

C

flip-flops

D

jeans

E

sunhat

F

jumper

2 Copy the diagram. Write or draw things you like to do in each kind of weather. The overlapping part shows things you like doing in both kinds of weather.

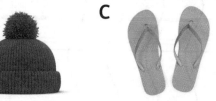

Hot weather   Cold weather

Observe and infer

3 How does temperature affect the weather? Work in groups.
Prepare a short play or dance to show how changing temperatures
cause wind and rain. Use the information in this picture and what
you learnt in class about the water cycle.

The Sun's rays heat the Earth

Condensation

Movement of cool air blows the clouds

As the air rises, it expands and cools

Cool air holds less water than warm air

Warm air rises

Evaporation

Land heats up faster than surface water

Cool air from over the water flows in

Interpret and measure

4   Look at this labelled diagram of a thermometer. Answer the
    questions about using a thermometer.

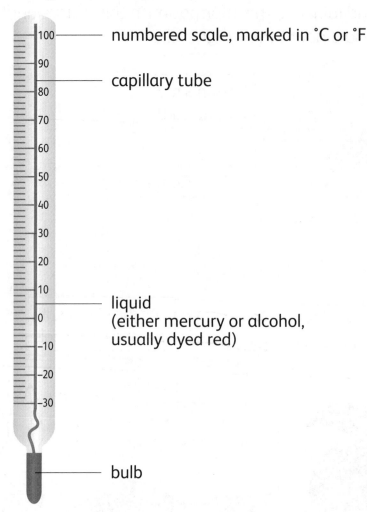

a   What does °C and °F mean?

b   How do you read the temperature from the thermometer?

c   What happens to the thermometer when the air gets warmer?

d   What happens when the air gets cooler?

5   Your teacher will bring a thermometer to class. Use the thermometer
    to measure the temperature of:

a   the air in the classroom

b   a cup of hot water

c   a glass of iced water.

6 Meteorology is the study of weather. Weather charts use meteorological symbols. These are simple pictures that show information about weather conditions.

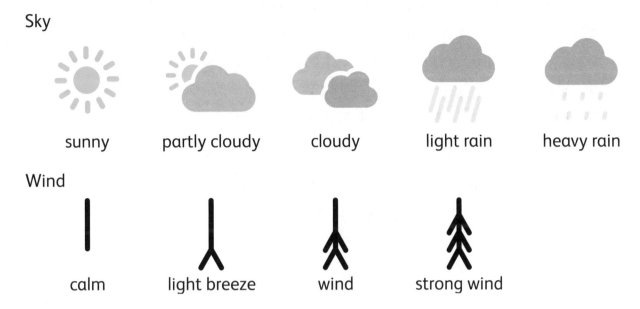

Look at this weather chart and answer the questions.

Monday	Tuesday	Wednesday	Thursday	Friday
21 °C	25 °C	24 °C	22 °C	23 °C

a   Which days were sunny?

b   Which day was coolest?

c   Which day had the most rain?

d   True or false? The day with the most rain was the warmest.

e   Describe the weather on Monday.

What did you learn?

1   Each statement is incorrect. Correct it by replacing the incorrect terms.
   a   We measure temperature using a rain gauge.
   b   The mercury in a thermometer rises when the temperature goes down.
   c   Temperature measures how wet something is.
   d   We measure temperature in degrees Celsius or Farringdon.
   e   Meteorology is the study of meteors.

2   Changes in temperature can make the wind blow. Explain why.

3   Which thermometer shows the temperature on a normal day
    in the Caribbean? Explain your answer.

A   55 °C   B   22 °C   C   10 °C

4   This weather chart gives
    information about weather
    conditions over three days.
    a   Which day was the windiest?
    b   Which day was the warmest?
    c   Choose one day and describe
        what the chart tells you about
        conditions on that day.

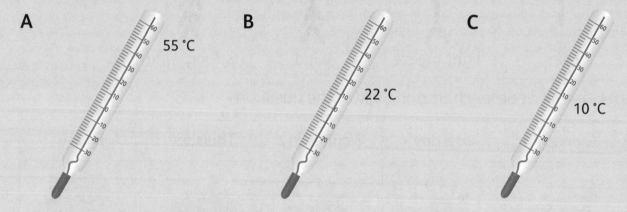

Monday	Tuesday	Wednesday
19 °C	24 °C	25 °C

Topic 2 Review

Key ideas and concepts

1 Copy this mind map. Fill in the five elements of weather. Around each element, write words we use to describe that weather element when people ask us about the weather on a particular day.

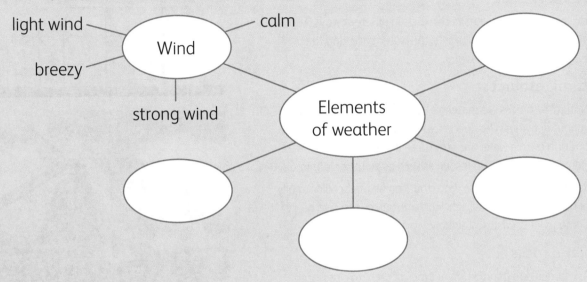

2 Write a term for each definition:

   a   the process of water turning from liquid to gas

   b   the process of water vapour turning from gas to liquid

   c   formations in the sky made out of many tiny water droplets

   d   the name we give to rain and dew.

Think, talk, write ...

1 Draw and label a sketch of an anemometer. Write a sentence to say what it does.

2 Make a poster of the water cycle.

3 Explain how changes in temperature can cause the wind to blow.

Quick check

1 Write down three ways in which wind can help us. Then write down three ways in which wind can be harmful.

2 Draw the symbols we would use to record these weather conditions:

   a   a sunny day with no wind, temperature of 19 degrees Celsius

   b   a rainy day with strong wind, temperature of 22 degrees Celsius.

Earth's resources

Teaching notes

Prior knowledge

✳ In Level 2, students classified objects in different ways. They also learnt about air pollutants, the water cycle, and the properties and uses of water.

Natural resources

✳ Natural resources are materials from nature that we use for various activities. The three most important resources for life on Earth are air, water and soil. These are non-living resources. Humans also use living resources such as plants and animals.

✳ Renewable resources are those that can be replaced naturally or used again. However, renewable resources can also be damaged if used unsustainably.

Soil and rocks

✳ Ask students to bring different types of rocks to class, or to collect pictures of rocks. They can sort rocks in different ways: by size, lustre or texture, and so on.

✳ For the design project, you will need stones, paint, glue and decorative materials. For the soil classification work, you will need jars and samples of soil from different areas.

Air as a resource

✳ Although air is invisible, it is all around us, and it has many properties. It is tasteless, odourless and colourless. It takes up space and has weight. It exerts force.

✳ You can decide how many of the activities in this unit to do, depending on the materials available in your classroom. You can also show YouTube videos of similar experiments and investigations.

Water as a resource

✳ Revise the water cycle before this unit. You will need bottles and samples of various kinds of water for the investigation of hard and soft water.

✳ Prepare the substances for the investigation into using water as a solvent. Make sure that you investigate some things that do and don't dissolve.

A

What are natural resources? Which natural resources are people using in these pictures? Which natural resources do you think we will use in future?

B

What does this bridge have in common with mountains, gravel, river pebbles and diamonds? What other items could you add to this list?

C

What fills the balloons and gives the balloons their shape? What happens if you overfill a balloon? What force is working here?

D

Why do we use water for washing dishes and clothes? What special properties does water have that makes it suitable for washing? Which products need water to make them work?

Think, talk and write

A Natural resources

(pages 28–30)

1 Copy this table. Write two ways that we use each of these natural resources.

Air	Soil	Rocks

B Soil and rocks

(pages 31–34)

1 What is the difference between sand and garden soil?

2 Draw and describe two different rocks found in your local area.

C Air as a resource

(pages 35–39)

1 You can't see clean air. How can you prove that there is air around you right now?

2 Besides breathing, what else do we use air for?

D Water as a resource

(pages 40–42)

1 Write down five ways in which you use water in your home.

A Natural resources

Explain

Water, air and soil are the three most important **natural resources** for all life on Earth. Natural resources are materials that we use from our natural environment. Coal, oil and natural gas are **non-renewable** resources. There is a **finite** amount of these resources on Earth. Once they are finished, we cannot make more. Some resources are **renewable**. **Solar** energy and wind are examples of renewable resources. No matter how much we use, they do not run out. **Sustainable** means using something in a way that can continue without damaging it. It is important to use natural resources sustainably.

Science ideas

In this unit you will:
* identify and describe some of the Earth's resources
* classify resources as renewable and non-renewable.

Key words

natural resources
non-renewable
finite   renewable
solar   sustainable

Observe and communicate

1 **a** Identify the natural resource that people are using in each picture.

   b Suggest what we use this resource for.

   c Say what would happen if it ran out.

A

B

C

D

E

2 **a** Draw pictures of three more natural resources.

   b Write what we use them for.

Classify and communicate

3 Water is a very important resource. Dan made a word cloud to show the ways his family uses water. The biggest words show the activities that use the most water.

washing machine

toilet   **bath**   garden   shower

sink   leaks   other   dishwasher

swimming pool washing the car

Design your own word cloud or draw a picture to show the main ways people use water in your home.

4 Classify each resource as renewable or non-renewable. Draw a poster that explains the difference between renewable and non-renewable resources, and illustrate it with these examples.

A Forests

B Rivers

C Fish

D Wind

E Solar energy

F Oil

G Soil

Infer

5 Even though some resources are renewable, we will damage them if we do not use them sustainably. In a group, choose one of these renewable resources: soil, water or air. Discuss how people damage this resource when they use it unsustainably.

What did you learn?

1   Which one is not a natural resource in each list?

   a   wind   water   sunlight   houses
   b   bees   planes   fish   birds

2   For each product, suggest a natural resource that was used to make it.

3   a   What is the difference between a renewable and non-renewable resource?
    b   Choose an example of a renewable resource and explain the difference between using it sustainably and unsustainably.

4   List three ways we use land as a natural resource.

B Soil and rocks

Science ideas

In this unit you will:

* describe ways we use rocks in our environment
* outline how soils are made from a variety of rocks
* design and make ornaments from rocks
* classify soils as sand, clay and loam.

Explain

The surface of the Earth, the **crust**, is made up of rocks. Rock is a very hard, solid substance made up of many different kinds of **minerals**. We use rocks in many different ways – for building, design and technology. A **stone quarry** is a place where we excavate earth to get rocks for building materials. **Soil** is an important resource for plant life and for farming. Soil is a mixture of different components: sand, humus, silt, gravel and clay. We classify soils as **sand**, **clay** or **loam**, depending on the soil **composition**.

Describe

1   Describe different kinds of rocks. Look at the different pictures of stones and rocks. For each picture describe the size, shape and appearance of the stone.
   * Is it small, medium or large?
   * Is it shiny or dull?
   * What colours can you see?

Key words

crust	sand
minerals	clay
stone quarry	loam
soil	composition

2 What can you see in these pictures? Talk about the different ways people use rocks.

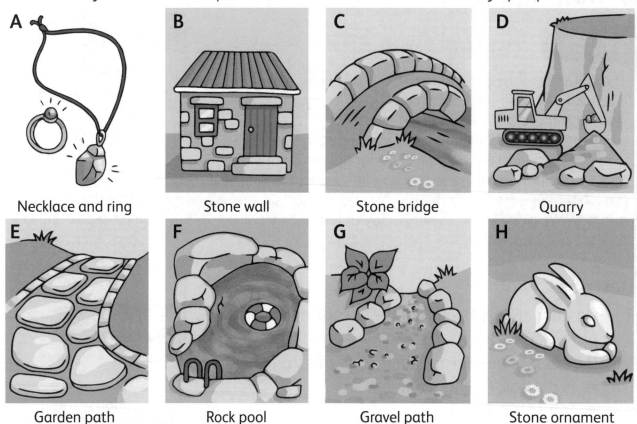

A	B	C	D
Necklace and ring	Stone wall	Stone bridge	Quarry

E	F	G	H
Garden path	Rock pool	Gravel path	Stone ornament

Design and make

Make a rock paperweight

The design brief
Make an animal paperweight from a stone.

You will need: smooth stones, paint, glue, small objects such as shells, beads, sequins or glitter for glueing.

Step 1: Think and plan
Think about how you will glue, paint and decorate your stones to create an animal.

Step 2: Design
Draw a design to show what you will use to make your paperweight.

Step 3: Make your animal
Use glue, paint and decorations to make your stone animal.

The main components of soil are sand, silt and clay. Soil may also contain gravel and humus.

A	B	C	D	E

Stones and gravel are small pieces of rock.	Sand is finely crushed rock. It does not hold water.	Silt is finer than sand. It mixes with water to make mud.	Clay has very tiny particles. It gets very sticky when it is wet.	Humus is crumbly, broken-down plant matter. It does not hold water.

Most soils are a mixture of all these components. We classify soil as sandy, loamy or clay, depending on which component makes up most of the mixture.

Infer and classify

3 Use the pictures and information on this page and discuss each description with a partner. Match each description to a type of soil.

   A This type of soil is very fine and dry and does not hold water well. It looks greyish when it is dry. It can't hold much water because the water runs through the large particles.

   B This type of soil gets waterlogged in the wet season because the fine particles stick together when they mix with water.

   C This type of soil has a balance of sand, silt, humus and clay. Medium-sized spaces between the particles allow the soil to hold the right amount of water so that plants can grow.

Sandy soil

Loamy soil

Clay soil

Investigate

Investigate soil composition

Sand   Loam   Clay

Step 1: Prepare
Put 1 cup of soil and 1 cup of water into a large jar. Close the jar and shake well.

Step 2: Wait
Leave the mixture to settle overnight.

water   water   water

clay
silt

silt   clay   silt   clay
sand   sand   sand

Step 3: Observe
The next day, look at your jar. The components should appear as layers, with the sand at the bottom, then silt, then clay.

* The water will rise to the top, because the other components are heavier.

* Gravel and stones usually sink to the bottom as they are heaviest. Humus will settle on top of the clay layer.

Observe and compare

4   You need two glass jars with lids.

   a   Collect samples of soils from two different places. Put each sample in a different jar.

   b   Describe the appearance of the soils. Look at the colour, texture and anything else you notice about it.

What did you learn?

1   Name three different ways we use rocks.

2   List these components of soil in order of particle size, from finest to largest:

    sand   clay   silt   gravel

C Air as a resource

Explain

The Earth's surface is covered in a layer of gases called the **atmosphere**. The atmosphere is made of **air** – a mixture of nitrogen, **oxygen**, water and some other gases.

All living things need air for **respiration**. Humans and animals use the oxygen from the air to **breathe**. Most plants also produce oxygen and release it into the atmosphere.

Air holds water. The atmosphere around us makes it possible for water to evaporate, form clouds, and then fall again as rain. Without air, we would not have a water cycle.

The atmosphere **insulates** the Earth. Heat from the Sun gets trapped in the atmosphere. This is how the Earth stays warm at night and **regulates** the temperature on Earth. That means the temperature does not get too hot or too cold.

Air also protects the Earth from meteors. Meteors are rocks that fall into the atmosphere from space. Most of these rocks burn up as they come into contact with the gases in the atmosphere.

Science ideas

In this unit you will:
* discuss the importance of air
* identify properties of air
* learn about the force that air exerts
* explore how air affects falling objects.

Key words

atmosphere	insulate
air	regulate
oxygen	air pressure
respiration	resistance
breathe	

Discuss

Look at the pictures and read the information. Discuss each picture in your group. Make a list of the ways in which air is important for life on Earth.

Investigate

Investigate some properties of air

Properties are special characteristics of a material and tell us how it behaves.
For example, clean air is colourless, odourless (has no smell) and tasteless.

1   You will need: a glass, tissue paper, a clear plastic bowl with water,
    a ping pong ball or small plastic toy that floats.

    a   Put the ball or toy into the water.

    b   Put the glass over the ball and push it down into the water. Observe:

        ✳ What happens to the ball?

        ✳ And to the air in the glass?

    c   Remove the glass from the water. Crumple the tissue paper and push it
        into the glass. Repeat part b. This time, also observe what happens to the
        tissue paper.

A
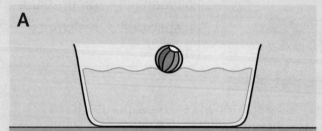

B

    d   ✳ Why do the ball and tissue paper not get wet?
        ✳ Why does the water move up in the bowl?
        ✳ What property of air does this investigation show?

2   You will need: 2 balloons, a thin wire or plastic
    clothes hanger, string or wire.

    a   Blow up the balloons and attach them
        to each end of a thin hanger using string
        or wire.

    b   ✳ What happens to the hanger when you
           deflate one balloon?

Both balloons
are blown up.

The blue
balloon has
been deflated.

        ✳ What property of air does this
           investigation show?

3 Discuss your results. Which two properties are not properties of air?

| colourless | tasteless | can push or pull things | odourless | takes up space |

| has weight | can move | heavier than water | occurs as solid, liquid or gas |

Investigate

Air exerts pressure. You know that air is made up of a mixture of gases and that it takes up space and has mass. Even though you can't feel it, air is pushing on us all the time. This is called **air pressure** – the air is pushing down on the Earth.

Try some of these ways to investigate air pressure:

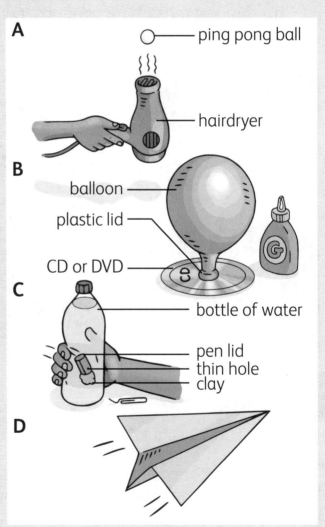

A — ping pong ball, hairdryer

B — balloon, plastic lid, CD or DVD

C — bottle of water, pen lid, thin hole, clay

D

1 Hold a hairdryer up and turn it on. Put a ping pong ball where the air is blowing. What happens? Why?

2 Glue a bottle cap to a CD. Put it on a flat surface. Blow up a balloon and carefully stretch it over the bottle cap, then let go. What happens? Why?

3 Put a blob of clay over the open end of a pen lid. Use a paper clip to make a thin hole through to the air inside the pen lid. Put it into a bottle of water. Close the bottle with its cap. Squeeze the bottle to make the lid sink to different levels. What is happening?

4 Make paper jets. Observe how they fly. What makes them stay up?

Investigate and compare

Resistance is a force that pushes against a moving object. Think about what happens when you try to open a car door in a strong wind. The wind pushes against the door, making it hard to open. Air resistance is a force that air exerts against things that are moving in the air.

1   Compare what happens when you drop two different objects from a height of 2 metres above the floor. Try these objects:
*   a pen and a sheet of paper
*   a large piece of paper and a small piece of paper
*   two pieces of paper the same size.
   a   Record your observations.
   b   Suggest reasons for your observations.

2   How are people using air resistance in each picture?

A

B

C

Design and make

Investigate how air can affect the rate of falling objects.

The challenge:
Find out how to make an object fall as slowly as possible.
Work on your own or in pairs.

You will need: a plastic figure, different kinds of paper or plastic (tissue paper, coffee filters, newspaper, construction paper, paper plates, paper towels, cellophane, plastic wrap), different types of thread or string (cotton, wool, string, dental floss, fishing line), tape, and a timer with millisecond counter.

Design:
Design a parachute that will make the plastic figure fall as slowly as possible. Draw a picture of your design, and note the materials you want to use.

Make:
Make your parachute. Every group or student needs to make a parachute for the same plastic figure.

Plan your test:
* Decide where you will test your parachutes.
* Decide from what height you need to start each drop.
* Check what else you need to do to make sure the test is fair.

Observe and record:
First, drop the plastic figure without a parachute. Note how long it takes to fall. Next, each student gets a chance to try their parachute with the plastic figure. Observe and record how long each drop takes.

What did you learn?

1   Describe three reasons why air is important for life on Earth.

2   How can we show that air takes up space?

3   How can we show that air exerts force?

D Water as a resource

Explain

Plants and animals need water to stay alive. Did you know that more than half of your body is made up of water? You can survive more than a month without food, but only a few days without water. There are many other ways in which we use water.

A

Farming crops

B

Washing clothes

C

Putting out a fire

D

Washing ourselves

E

Transporting cargo

F

Snorkelling and kayaking

Interpret and infer

1 a How does each picture tell us something about the importance of the water cycle to people?

   b How do people use water for transportation?

   c What activities can you think of that people do in water?

2   You already know about the **water cycle**. Copy and complete
    the diagram of the water cycle. Label it correctly.

precipitation

surface water

evaporation

condensation

clouds   Sun

heat

3   Are some parts of the water cycle more important than others?
    Give reasons for your answers. Compare answers with a partner
    and explain why you agree or disagree with their answer.

Investigate and record

What dissolves in water?
Water is a **solvent**. This is an important property. It means that many other substances
dissolve easily in water. **Solubility** is the ability of a substance to dissolve in water.

You will need: glass jars, teaspoons, substances for testing.

Gravel   Sugar   Salt   Talcum powder

Soap   Marbles (glass)   Aluminium (metal)   Paper

1   Guess which of these substances will dissolve in water and which will not.

2   Test each substance for solubility. Record your observations.

Investigate

Hard and soft water

When you use soap with water, the soap forms white foamy suds. This is called lathering. As water moves through the ground, or through water pipes, minerals can dissolve into the water. **Hard water** is water that contains high quantities of dissolved minerals. It is called hard water because it does not **lather** well with soap. Water with low levels of minerals is called **soft water**.

You will need: five 500-ml water bottles, dishwashing liquid, labels and markers, a ruler.

Step 1: Collect

Collect samples of five different kinds of water, if you can: rain water, river water, tap water, sea water and spring water. Fill each bottle halfway with the water sample. Label each bottle.

Step 2: Add soap

Add three drops of dishwashing liquid to each bottle. Close the lid tightly.

Step 3: Shake

Shake each bottle for 15 seconds.

Step 4: Measure

Measure the height of the suds in each bottle.

1   Which bottle had the most suds?

2   Which bottle had the least suds?

What did you learn?

1   Make up a song or poem about the importance of the water cycle to human life.

2   Draw pictures of ways we use water as a solvent in our food and drinks.

3   Explain the difference between hard and soft water.

Topic 3 Review

Key ideas and concepts

1 Identify the resource shown in each picture.

2 Write this list of materials in order from the material with the smallest particles to the material with the biggest pieces.

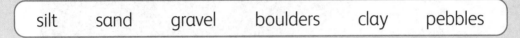

silt   sand   gravel   boulders   clay   pebbles

3 Write or draw three different things people make or build from rocks or stones.

Think, talk, write …

1 Name two renewable resources and two non-renewable resources.

2 Explain why it is important to use renewable resources.

3 Name the three main types of soil, and say which one is best for growing plants.

4 Describe one experiment you did to show air resistance or pressure.

Quick check

1 What are the three most important resources for life on Earth?

2 What happens when you mix soil and water in a jar and shake it, and then leave it? Why would you do this?

3 Why is seawater not good for washing?

4 How does each product use water's property as a solvent?

A

What does this picture show?

Teaching notes

Prior knowledge

✳ Ask students to name the heavenly bodies they know about in space (Moon, planets, Earth, stars, and so on).

✳ Ask which of these they have seen with their own eyes, and which they have seen in books, videos, or elsewhere.

The solar system

✳ If possible, bring books or pictures of the solar system to class.

✳ There are many videos on YouTube that introduce the Earth, Moon and Sun, as well as information on the movements of the solar system.

Think, talk and write

A **The solar system**
   (pages 45–48)

People used to believe that the Earth was at the centre of the universe, and the Sun, Moon and other planets moved around us. How do you think scientists worked out that this was incorrect?

A The solar system

Explain

The Earth is one of the eight **planets** in our **solar system**. The Sun is the closest **star** to the Earth. A star is a massive, burning ball of gas. The Earth **rotates** on its own axis. All the planets **revolve** around the Sun. Each planet travels in its own **orbit**. The Moon is a **satellite** of the Earth.

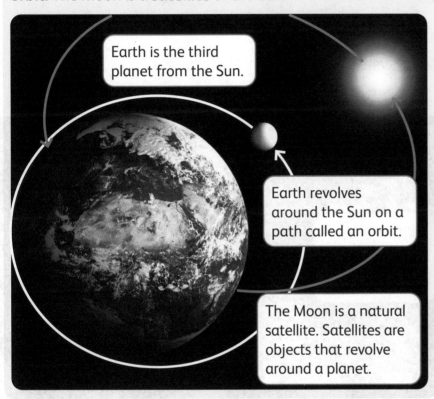

Earth is the third planet from the Sun.

Earth revolves around the Sun on a path called an orbit.

The Moon is a natural satellite. Satellites are objects that revolve around a planet.

Science ideas

In this unit you will:
* learn about the relationship between the Earth, Moon and Sun
* understand how this relationship affects humans
* define the terms rotate, revolve, planet, star and satellite
* identify components of the solar system.

Key words

planet
solar system
star
rotate
revolve
orbit
satellite

Research

1   Work in groups of three. Arrange yourselves as the Earth, Moon and Sun. Show how:
   * the Earth rotates on its axis
   * the Moon revolves around the Earth
   * the Earth revolves around the Sun.

2   Which of these three movements creates night and day on Earth?

3   Use books or the internet to find out the names of some human-made satellites that travel around the Earth and other planets.

Hypothesise

4   What would happen if …? Think about how the relationship between the Earth, Sun and Moon affects our lives. Work in pairs or groups. Choose one of the topics below. Prepare a short presentation or video about what would happen if:

   ✳ the Earth started moving closer to the Sun
   ✳ the Earth started moving further away from the Sun
   ✳ the Moon disappeared.

Interpret and communicate

5   The components of the solar system are the Sun, the planets and their satellites.

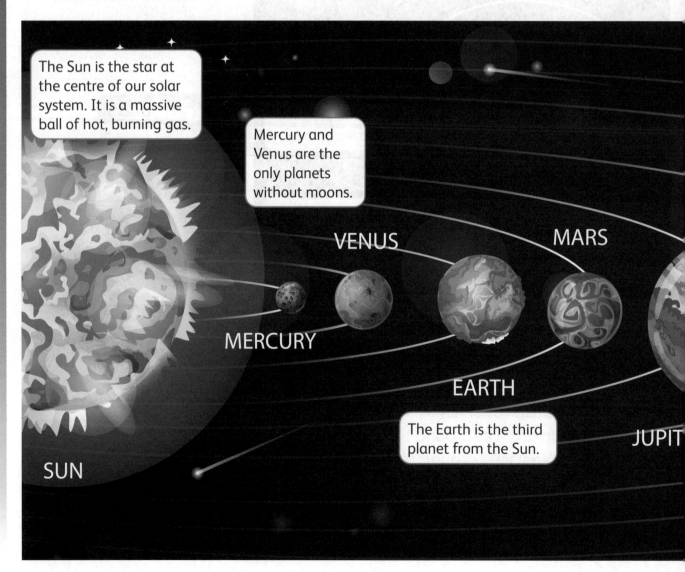

6 For each definition, find the term that matches correctly.

  a To turn about its own axis

  b To move on a path around another object

  c A celestial body that is lit by a star

  d A burning ball of hot gases

  e An object that moves around a planet

7 Make a booklet about the components of the solar system. Draw and write one page about each planet, and a page each for the Moon and Sun. Include pictures and information about each component. You can use books and the internet to research the information.

What did you learn?

Identify the incorrect statement under each picture.

A

The Sun is the closest star to Earth.
The Sun is the centre of the solar system.
The Sun moves around the planets.

B

The Earth is a planet.
The Earth is the biggest planet.
The Earth has one moon.

C

There is one moon in the solar system.
The Moon revolves around the Earth.
The Moon is a satellite.

D

Saturn is a planet that has large, bright rings.
Saturn is one of the Earth's satellites.
Saturn moves around the Sun in a bigger orbit than Earth's orbit.

E

Stars can be suns in other solar systems.
Stars are burning balls of gas.
Stars are also planets.

F

When our side of the Earth faces the Sun, it is daytime.
When our side of the Earth turns away from the Sun, it is night-time.
At night, we get our light and heat from the Moon.

Topic 4 Review

Key ideas and concepts

1   Look at this sketch of the solar system. Write what each letter represents.

2   What do the curved lines in the sketch show?

3   Why is the Moon not a planet?

4   Why is the Sun not a planet?

Think, talk, write …

1   Explain how you know the Earth is turning on its axis each day. What can you see each day that shows you that this is true?

2   Earth is the third planet from the Sun. Why do you think this position is important for life on Earth?

3   Solar means 'to do with the Sun'. Why do you think scientists called our group of planets a solar system?

Quick check

1   What are the three components of the solar system?

2   Define these terms:
    a   revolve
    b   rotate
    c   star
    d   satellite.

3   Name:
    a   the planet we live on
    b   the closest planet to the Sun
    c   the planet furthest from the Sun
    d   the biggest planet
    e   the Earth's natural satellite.

A

Teaching notes

Prior knowledge

* Students should be able to identify and name some local plants and know the difference between trees, shrubs, vines and herbs. They should be able to identify different kinds of leaves and say how we use leaves in everyday life.

Parts of plants

* Most plants have roots, stems, leaves and flowers.

* Plants take in water and nutrients through their roots. These move up through the stem to reach all the parts of the plant.

* Leaves are the food factories of the plant. The leaves absorb sunlight and use it to produce energy (food).

* The flowers of plants are important for reproduction.

Classifying and comparing plants

* Plants are classified as flowering or non-flowering. Flowering plants make seeds, non-flowering plants do not.

* Flowering plants are monocotyledons or dicotyledons. Mono means single: monocotyledons have seeds with only one part. Di means two: dicotyledons have two-part seeds. Cotyledons is the name for seed parts.

* Monocotyledonous and dicotyledonous plants have distinguishing features. For example, monocots such as corn have fibrous roots, jointed stems and leaves with parallel veins. Dicots such as beans have tap roots, unjointed stems and leaves with a network of veins.

Plant propagation

* Propagation is the process of making new plants from existing plants.

* Some plants propagate themselves naturally by growing runners or making new plants from their leaves. This is called vegetative propagation (or reproduction) because it doesn't involve seeds.

* Plants can also be propagated by planting seeds. Flowering plants produce seeds that can germinate (start to grow) if the conditions are right.

* Seeds need water, the right temperature (warmth) and a suitable location (for example, fertile soil) to germinate.

Name all the plant parts that you can see in this photograph.

Which parts of the plant are usually above the ground?

What do the roots do for the plant?

Have you seen plants growing in places other than soil?

B

This is a flowering plant. Describe the flowers.

Which other plants do you know that make flowers?

Some plants do not have flowers. Can you think of any that don't flower?

C

This kalanchoe plant is sometimes called 'mother of millions'. Why do you think it was given this name?

What is growing on the edges of the leaves? What happens when these fall off?

D

This plant is growing next to a road.

Can you find its seeds?

The seed pods dry out and split open. Some seeds fall onto the tar road and some are eaten by birds. Which seeds do you think will grow?

Think, talk and write

A Parts of plants (pages 52–54)

Fill in the missing words. They are all parts of plants.

1 Spinach is the _____ of the spinach plant.
2 Bananas are the _____ of the banana tree.
3 Orchids are _____.
4 The trunk is the _____ of the coconut tree.
5 The _____ of hibiscus bushes grow underground.
6 Beans are the _____ of bean plants.

B Classifying plants (pages 55–60)

1 Find some grass growing at school. Uproot a plant carefully and put it on some newspaper.
2 Compare your grass plant to the one in photograph B.
    a How do the leaves, stem and roots differ from those in the photograph?
    b Do grasses have flowers and seeds? How do you know this?

C Growing new plants (pages 61–65)

1 The seeds of many plants are found inside the fruits of the plant. Make a list of plants you know that have:
    a one seed inside the fruit
    b many seeds inside the fruit
    c seeds on the outside of the fruit.

D Will it grow? (pages 66–69)

Which seeds do you think will grow? Why?

1 A seed on a dish in the fridge
2 A seed planted in sand and not given any water
3 A seed planted in garden soil, watered and placed in the sun

A Parts of plants

Plants have different parts. Each part has its own features. The **roots**, **stems**, **leaves**, **flowers**, **fruits** and **seeds** of plants have their own special **functions** that help the plant grow and survive.

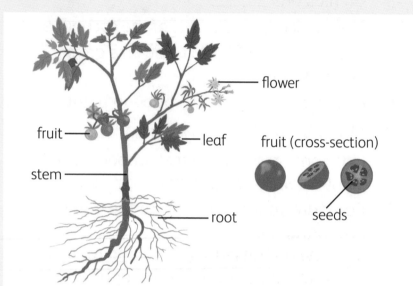

This table summarises the main functions of the different parts of plants.

Part of the plant	Function
Roots Most roots are underground.	Roots help to hold the plant in place. Roots take in water and food from the soil. Some roots store food for the plant.
Stem The stem of a tree is called the trunk.	The stem supports the plant and holds it up. Water and food from the roots are transported through the stem to the different parts of the plant.
Leaves	Leaves make food for the plant. They use sunlight to do this. Little openings in the leaves let air and water move into or out of the plant.
Flowers Many flowers have petals, but some do not.	The flowers make seeds. The colour and smell of the flowers attract pollinators, such as insects and birds. Flowers have to be pollinated before they can make seeds.

Science ideas

In this unit you will:
* revise what you already know about the parts of plants
* describe the features of parts of plants
* link the features of plant parts to their functions.

Key words

roots	fruits
stems	seeds
leaves	function
flowers	

Part of the plant	Function
Fruits Fruits are formed from flowers when the petals fall off.	The fruits protect the seeds. They also attract animals that help to spread the seeds.
Seeds	Seeds make new plants. Each seed contains food that the new plant uses to help it grow.

Interpret and record

1   Here are two different plants.

Plant A – Dandelion

Plant B – Hot pepper

   a   Sketch both plants in your book and label the parts of each.

   b   Where are the seeds of a pepper plant?

   c   What do dandelion seeds look like?

2   Most plant roots grow underground. Can you think of any plants whose roots are above the ground or in water?

Investigate and communicate

3   Look at some of the flowers on plants around your school.

   a   What type of animal do you think will pollinate each type?

   b   Try to find evidence to support your ideas. You could watch the flowers to see which insects or birds come to the plant. You could also ask gardeners or farmers, or find information in books or on the internet.

   c   Share what you learn with your group.

Infer

4   The main function of flowers is to attract animals (insects and birds) for pollination so the plant can make seeds. Read what each animal likes. Then decide which flower would attract it. Write the name of the animal and the name of the flower in your book.

> Bees: lots of pollen, sweet nectar
>
> Butterflies: bright colours, flat-topped flowers with short tubes, full sun
>
> Moths: active at night, white or pale flowers with strong scent
>
> Hummingbirds: orange, red and yellow colours, not attracted by scent, lots of sweet nectar, often in tubes
>
> Flies: dull or dark flowers, bad smells
>
> Midges: small flowers, fungus smells (mushrooms)

A

Pawpaw flowers are dark in colour and smell a bit like bread.

B

Moonflowers are white and they bloom at night. They have a strong scent.

C

Cocoa flowers grow low down on the trunk. They are small and face down. They smell a bit musty, like mushrooms.

D

Heliconia flowers produce lots of sticky sweet nectar in the tubes.

E

Lignum vitae (tree of life) flowers grow in clusters in the sun. They have shallow nectar tubes and flat tops.

F

Palm flowers produce lots of pollen and nectar.

What did you learn?

Make a presentation about plants and their parts.

* Make one slide or card for each part of the plant.
* Your slide or card should have the name of the part, pictures to show what this part looks like on different plants, and information about its function.

B Classifying plants

Sunflower

Orchid

In this unit you will:

* classify plants as flowering or non-flowering plants
* use the type of seeds that plants make to divide flowering plants into monocotyledons and dicotyledons
* describe the differences between monocotyledonous and dicotyledonous plants.

Key words

seed leaf	cotyledon
dicotyledons	
monocotyledons	
classify	flowering
non-flowering	

The Caribbean region is home to thousands of different kinds of plants, from simple algae to large trees. All plants have some similarities, but they also have differences. For example, some plants produce flowers, while others do not. Some plants make seeds and others do not. Plants that make flowers can have different kinds of seeds.

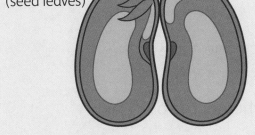

two cotyledons
(seed leaves)

This is a bean seed.

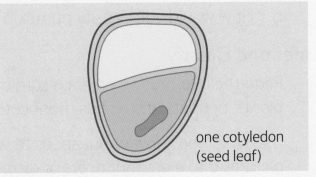

one cotyledon
(seed leaf)

This is a maize (corn) seed.

You can see that the bean seed has two parts. These are the **seed leaves** or **cotyledons**. Plants with seeds like these are called **dicotyledons**. We shorten this to dicots. Beans, sunflowers and apples are all dicots.

The corn seed only has one seed leaf. We call plants with seeds like these **monocotyledons**. We shorten this to monocots. Maize, wheat and orchids are monocots.

We can use the differences between plants to **classify** them and put them into different groups.

Classify

1   Work with a partner. Use the information in this diagram to answer
    questions about **flowering** and **non-flowering** plants.

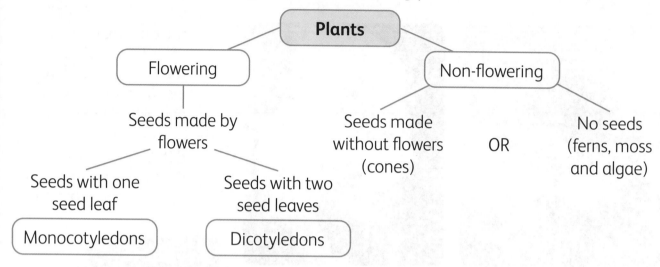

a   What are the two main groups of plants?
b   Give an example of a flowering plant in your area.
c   What type of plant is a pine tree?
d   How would you classify sea grass?
e   Do all plants that make seeds have flowers?
f   All grasses are monocots. What does this tell you about their seeds?
g   How would you classify pumpkin plants? Why?

Infer and classify

2   Read the information on each card on the next page. Classify the
    plants, peanuts and rice as monocots or dicots.

Use what you know about seeds to work out whether the plants in
pictures **a** to **e** are monocots or dicots.

a banana   b watermelon   c pawpaw   d coconut   e mango

A Peanut plants are interesting. The flowers appear above ground, but the seeds are formed in shells under the soil.

B Rice is a grain that grows in water. The rice grains you eat are actually the seeds of the rice plant.

C When monocotyledonous plants start growing, the first thing you see is a single spike, like a blade of grass, growing out of the ground. When dicotyledonous plants start growing, you see two leaves and the start of the stem.

Observe and record

3   Collect as many types of seeds as you can and bring them to class. Try to find at least some of these:

cocoa   peas   cashew   corn   sesame   wheat   avocado   watermelon   sunflower   pumpkin

a   Observe the outside of the seeds carefully. Draw a picture of each one and label it.

b   Place the seeds in a shallow bowl of water and leave them to soak overnight.

c   Remove the seeds from the water and place them on a dishtowel to dry.

d   Observe the inside of each seed. If the seed has a hard or leathery layer on the outside, gently peel it away so you can see the cotyledons.

e   Write monocot or dicot next to the drawing you made of each seed.

Characteristics of monocots and dicots

Explain

Monocotyledons and dicotyledons have different characteristics that can help you identify and classify them.

	Monocotyledons	Dicotyledons
Seeds	One cotyledon	Two cotyledons
Roots	Thin, stringy and fibrous	One strong central tap root with others branching off
Leaves	Often long and narrow Veins are parallel to each other	Often broad Veins are arranged in a branching network
Flowers	Petals often grouped in multiples of three	Petals often grouped in multiples of four or five

Observe and classify

4   Look at the pictures of these flowers carefully.

   a   How are the petals arranged in each flower?

   b   Decide whether each flower is a monocot or a dicot by counting the number of petals it has.

   c   Find three flowers that grow around your school. How would you classify the plants? Why?

5   Draw and label a typical monocotyledonous plant. Include the main parts of the plant in your drawing.

6   Find a leaf from a dicotyledonous plant. Stick it into your book. Sketch the veins of its leaf next to it.

Investigate and record

1   You will now investigate the plants that grow in and around your school to work out whether they are monocots or dicots. Work in groups to do this.

   a   Choose ten plants. Photograph or draw them. Name them if you can.

   b   Draw up a table like this one:

Monocotyledons	Dicotyledons

c Stick the photographs or drawings of the plants into the correct columns.

d Show your table to another group and check each other's tables to make sure the plants are classified correctly.

2 Which types of flowering plants are most common in and near your school?

> We need to respect and care for plants around us. Never disturb or dig up plants to look at their roots unless your teacher instructs you to do this. Take notes, make drawings or take photographs when you observe plants.

What did you learn?

1 Explain the meaning of each term in your own words:

   a classify   b cotyledon   c non-flowering.

2 Look at the plant in the photograph.

   a Is this a tree or a vine? How do you know?

   b Do you think this plant makes seeds? Give a reason for your answer.

   c Describe the flowers, fruits and leaves of this plant.

   d Classify the plant as a monocot or dicot. Give two reasons for your choice.

   e What would you expect the roots of this plant to look like? Why?

C Growing new plants

Explain

Propagation means increasing or multiplying. Plant propagation is the process of growing new plants.

Plants can propagate themselves in different ways.

You already know that plants with flowers make **seeds** and that these seeds can grow into new plants. Propagation using seeds is called **sexual reproduction** and this needs two parent plants to happen.

A mango tree grows from a mango seed. The mango flower had to be pollinated before it could form seeds.

Plants can also propagate by themselves without flowers and seeds. They do this by growing new plants from their stems, roots and leaves.

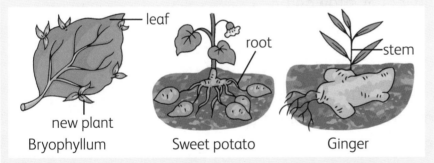

leaf	root	stem
new plant		
Bryophyllum	Sweet potato	Ginger

Plants that develop new plants on existing plant parts use **vegetative propagation** and only need one parent plant.

Science ideas

In this unit you will:

* find out how plants make new plants on their own (propagation)
* describe how plants can make new plants using vegetative propagation
* identify plants that grow from seeds and find out more about how they do this
* learn about the advantages and disadvantages of using seeds as a method to grow new plants.

Key words

propagation
seeds
sexual reproduction
vegetative propagation

This spider plant has made lots of new little spider plants on long stems. These little plants can be removed and put in soil. They will grow into adult spider plants.

Infer and predict

1 Mr Julien finds that some garlic in his store cupboard has started to make green shoots.

   a How would you explain to Mr Julien what is happening to the garlic?

   b Predict what will happen if you split the garlic and plant the sections in the soil.

   c Can you think of other vegetables that make shoots like this if you leave them in a dark cupboard for too long?

2 Look carefully at this strawberry plant.

   a What do the flowers and fruits tell you about this plant?

   b What do the little plants growing from the stem tell you about this plant?

   c Which method of propagation do you think is best for getting lots of strawberry plants quickly? Why?

Interpret and record

3 Look at these examples of vegetative propagation. Write a sentence to describe how each plant propagates itself.

A

Banana

B

Ginger

C

Mint

Investigate

You are now going to plant some seeds and observe them grow.
You will need:

recycled
containers to
use as plant
pots, with a hole
in the bottom

garden
soil

a ruler

seeds   peas

sunflower seeds   beans

plastic lids on
which pots
can stand

coconut
fibre

Follow these steps to plant the seeds.

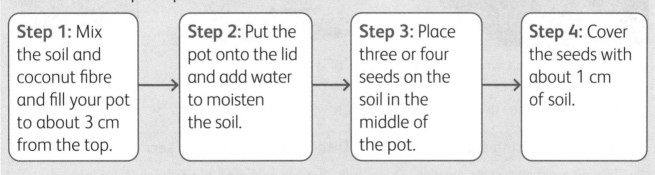

Step 1: Mix the soil and coconut fibre and fill your pot to about 3 cm from the top.

Step 2: Put the pot onto the lid and add water to moisten the soil.

Step 3: Place three or four seeds on the soil in the middle of the pot.

Step 4: Cover the seeds with about 1 cm of soil.

Your teacher will tell you where to place your pots.

Observe your pots every day. Water them if the soil looks dry.

Record how long it takes for the seedlings to appear above the soil.

When the seedlings are about 10 cm tall, pinch out the weaker ones, leaving only the strongest seedling in your pot.

Continue to water the plant as it grows.

If your school has a garden, you can transplant the seedlings and let them grow outside.

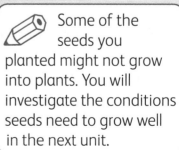
Some of the seeds you planted might not grow into plants. You will investigate the conditions seeds need to grow well in the next unit.

Seeds or vegetative propagation?

Explain

Some plants can be propagated both by using seeds and by vegetative propagation. When you want to grow plants, you have to think about which methods are most suitable for your needs and for the type of plants.

A

B

C

Geraniums can be grown by putting the stem of a plant into water, where it will grow roots. They can also be grown from seeds.

There are advantages and disadvantages to growing plants from seeds.

Advantages of using seeds	Disadvantages of using seeds
✳ It is an inexpensive method of growing a large number of plants. ✳ You don't need special equipment or tools. ✳ Seeds are easy to transport and most can be stored. ✳ Some plants can only be grown from seeds. Examples are lettuce and sunflowers.	✳ Some seeds don't store well (for example, carrot and onion seeds will die at room temperature). ✳ Some plants don't produce seeds that you can plant (for example, many types of bananas don't produce seeds). ✳ It takes a long time for plants to fully grow from seeds. ✳ Plants grown from seeds will be fully grown at different times, and this can be a problem for farmers who want to take crops to market at the same time.

Interpret and infer

4   Read each statement carefully. Do you agree? If not, how would you correct it?

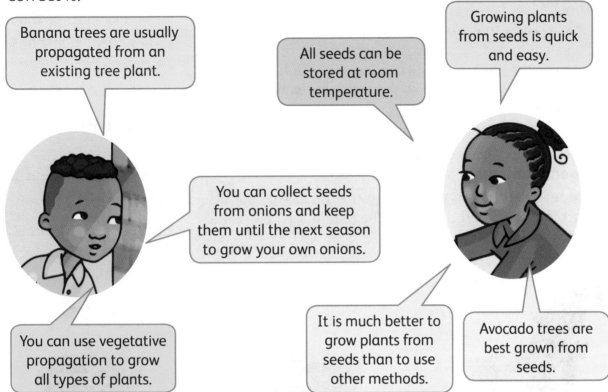

> Banana trees are usually propagated from an existing tree plant.

> All seeds can be stored at room temperature.

> Growing plants from seeds is quick and easy.

> You can collect seeds from onions and keep them until the next season to grow your own onions.

> You can use vegetative propagation to grow all types of plants.

> It is much better to grow plants from seeds than to use other methods.

> Avocado trees are best grown from seeds.

5   Mrs Johnson grows carrots and sunflowers, which she sells at the market. What methods of propagation do you think she uses? Why?

What did you learn?

1   Name two ways in which plants propagate themselves.

2   Match each plant to the method or methods to propagate it.

Lettuce Garlic Strawberry Sunflower Banana	Seeds
	Vegetative propagation

D Will it grow?

Explain

You already know that plants can grow from seeds. The baby plants are contained inside the seed, where they remain protected by the seed coat until conditions are right for them to start growing. Most seeds need warmth and water to start growing.

When conditions are right, the baby plant inside the seed starts to grow and break out of the seed coat. This process is called **germination**.

When a seed germinates, the first part to push its way out of the seed coat is the part that forms the root of the new plant. The stems and leaves follow.

Science ideas

In this unit you will:
* describe what happens when seeds germinate
* list the things that seeds need to germinate
* investigate how different conditions affect germination.

Key words

germination

This seed has not germinated yet. It has been planted in soil and watered.

After a few days, the seed starts to germinate. A small shoot has broken through the seed coat.

After a week, a small stem and leaves appear (sprout) above the soil. The roots develop a little more. This small plant is called a seedling.

Interpret and infer

1 Discuss these questions in your groups.

   a What conditions do seeds need to start germinating?

   b Why don't seeds germinate inside the packets sold at a store?

   c Plants need sunlight. Do you think seeds need light to germinate?

   d What is the difference between a seed and a seedling?

2 Look at this photo and answer the questions.

a What has happened to this seed?

b If you planted it in soil, which way up would you plant it? Why?

Infer and predict

3 A class did an experiment to see whether seeds need water to germinate.

a Read what they did.

We filled two egg trays with soil and
planted 24 beans in each tray.
Tray A was given 30 ml of water every day.
Tray B was given no water at all.
Both trays were placed in a warm spot in
the classroom.

We observed the trays every day and counted the number of seedlings that appeared above the soil.

We recorded our results in a table.

	Mon	Tues	Wed	Thurs	Fri	Mon	Tues	Wed
Tray A	0	0	0	0	2	5	9	16
Tray B	0	0	0	0	0	0	0	0

b What did they keep the same in the two trays? Why?

c What did they change?

d What do the results tell you?

e Predict what would happen if you started to water Tray B in the second week.

Experiment

Do an experiment to find out if seeds need warmth to germinate
You will now do an experiment to find out how germinating seeds are affected by temperature.

You will need: cotton wool or paper towels, two waterproof trays (plastic lids work well), six seeds (beans, peas or corn), water, dark bags (paper or plastic). Follow the steps to set up the seed germinating trays.

Step 1: Wet some cotton wool and put it on the trays. Place three seeds on each tray.

Step 2: Cover the seeds with another layer of wet cotton wool.

Step 3: Put both trays into a dark bag. Label them A and B.

Step 4: Place tray A in a cold place, such as a fridge or a cooler box.

Step 5: Place tray B in a warm place, like a windowsill.

Step 6: Leave the seeds for a week and observe them daily to see what happens.

1   What are you trying to find out in this experiment?

2   Why is it important to set up both trays in the same way?

3   Why do you need to put the trays into a dark bag?

4   Predict what you think will happen to the seeds. Why?

5   After a week, record your results in your book.

6   Were your predictions correct?

Predict

Will seeds still germinate if you freeze them or put them into boiling
water before you try to grow them?

7   What do you think will happen? Why?

8   Design an experiment to test your predictions and answer the question.

9   Record your ideas before you do your experiment. Use these headings:

> **Our experiment**
>
> **A**   Aim (What we want to find out)
>
> **B**   Hypothesis (Our prediction)
>
> **C**   Equipment (What we will use)
>
> **D**   Procedure (What we will do, step by step)
>
> **E**   Results (What happened)
>
> **F**   Conclusion (What we learnt from this)

Carry out your experiment and record your results.

What did you learn?

1   The diagram shows the stages in the life
     cycle of a squash plant.

   a   Write the letters A to G below each
        other in your book. Choose the word
        that describes each stage from the
        box and write it next to the letter.

   > ripe fruit with seeds   planting
   >   pollination   fruits form
   > germination   sprout forms   seedling

   b   Write a sentence next to each stage to
        describe what happens in that stage.

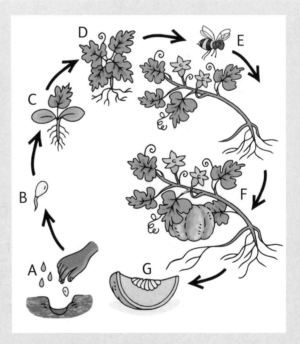

2   There is no water or air on the Moon. Do you think plants could
     grow there? Explain your answer.

Topic 5 Review

Key ideas and concepts

Design a leaflet with words and pictures to summarise what you learnt about plants in this topic. Fold a piece of paper into thirds and use these headings for your summary.

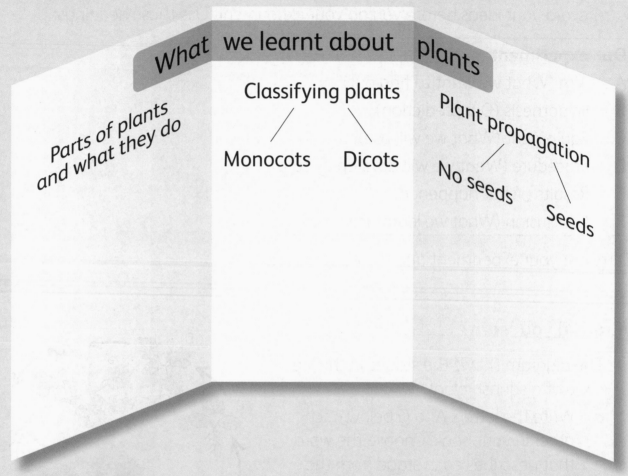

Think, talk, write ...

1 Make a list of the vegetables your family eats.

2 For each vegetable, say whether you are eating a root, stem, leaf, flower or seed. For example, callaloo – leaves; carrots – roots.

3 Many animals eat plant seeds. How does this help plants propagate themselves?

4 How can the number of petals in a flower tell you what kind of plant it is?

Quick check

1 Study the diagram and answer the questions.

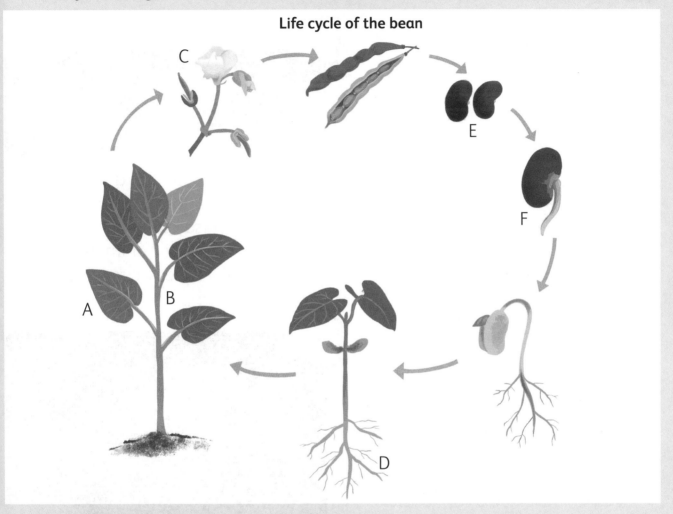

Life cycle of the bean

a Name the parts of the plant labelled A, B C and D.
b What is the function of each part?
c What type of seed is shown at E?
d Name another type of seed and say how it differs from this one.
e What has happened to the seed at F?
f What conditions are needed for the seed to do this (F)?

2 Bean plants are propagated from seeds.
a What is it called when plants grow from other plant parts?
b Give two examples of plants that can propagate themselves without seeds.

Teaching notes

Prior knowledge

* Students should know the characteristics of living things. They should by now have classified animals in different ways. The names and characteristics of some local animals should be familiar to them.

Classifying animals

* Scientists classify animals in different ways, but all animals can be grouped as vertebrates or invertebrates. Vertebrates are animals with an internal skeleton made of bones. They all have a backbone (spine) made of vertebrae.

* Vertebrates can be further divided into five classes. These are: mammals, birds, reptiles, fish and amphibians.

* At this stage, students name the classes and learn about some of the features of the animals found in these classes. It is useful to have pictures and information about local animals.

External features and their functions

* In biology, we study the features of animals (the structure) and learn what these features do (their functions).

* At this level, focus on external features (those that are on the outside of the body), so look at movement, responses to the environment (hiding and staying safe) and feeding.

* It isn't possible to learn about every single animal. Rather, try to teach students to describe the features they observe and to infer their functions. Some features are obvious (for example, birds use their wings to fly), but there are also birds that don't fly (penguins and ostriches), so it is important to teach students to think critically and to consider what else they know about animals to help them investigate and answer questions.

A

These are the remains of a dead animal.
* What animal do you think this was? Why do you say so?
* Can you classify all animals by their remains? Give a reason for your answer.

B

This is a scorpion fish, which lives on coral reefs. Which body parts help the fish swim away quickly when it is disturbed? What makes it difficult to see this fish on the reef? Scorpion fish have spines on their back, which are poisonous. How do these spines help protect it? What should you do if you stand on a scorpion fish?

C

This osprey is eating fish. How do you think the bird caught and killed the fish? How is the bird's beak suited to eating fish?

Think, talk and write

A **Classifying animals** (pages 74–76)

1 In each group below, one animal doesn't belong. Find the animal that doesn't belong and say why it doesn't belong.

Group A: grouper	red snapper	conch	parrot fish
Group B: seagull	dove	pelican	fruit bat
Group C: tree frog	cane toad	whistling frog	iguana
Group D: loggerhead turtle	octopus	lizard	tree boa
Group E: dog	cat	chicken	mouse

2 Suggest one more animal that does belong in each group.

B **Body parts for moving, hiding and protection** (pages 77–80)

1 For each animal, say what body parts it uses to move around.
   a Seagull
   b Tortoise
   c Dog

C **Body parts for finding food and eating** (pages 81–84)

Imagine you are a parrot. Answer these questions.

1 What do you eat?
2 How do you find food?
3 You don't have hands. How do you hold your food?

A Classifying animals

Explain

Scientists classify animals by putting them into groups that have similar features. One way of classifying animals is by whether or not they have a bony skeleton with a backbone.

Vertebrates have a backbone. These animals also have other bones and their skeleton is inside their bodies.

These animals are all vertebrates.

All other animals are **invertebrates**. These animals do not have a backbone. Here are some invertebrates that you might have seen.

There are five main groups, or classes, of vertebrates.

Science ideas

In this unit you will:

* understand and use the terms vertebrates and invertebrates
* know that fish, birds, reptiles, amphibians and mammals are all groups of vertebrates.

Key words

vertebrates
invertebrates
birds
fish
mammals
reptiles
amphibians

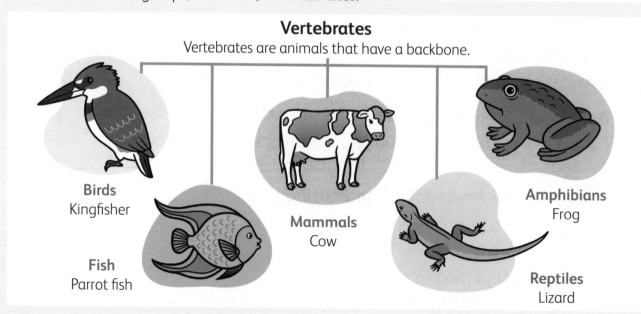

Vertebrates
Vertebrates are animals that have a backbone.

Birds
Kingfisher

Fish
Parrot fish

Mammals
Cow

Reptiles
Lizard

Amphibians
Frog

Classify and record

1 You are now going to classify some animals.

a Draw a diagram like this in your book:

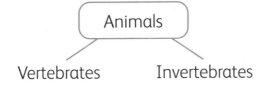

Vertebrates   Invertebrates

b Classify these sea animals as vertebrates or invertebrates. Write the animal names under the correct heading on your diagram.

c Add the name of one more sea animal to each group.

2   Read the descriptions.

A

These animals have moist, slimy skin. They are found in and out of water, but they lay their eggs in water.

B

These animals have skin with hair or fur. They give birth to live young. Humans belong in this group.

C

These animals have feathers and wings but they don't all fly. They have beaks and they lay eggs.

D

These animals have dry skin with scales. They lay their eggs on land and may bury them.

E

These animals live and breathe in water. They have scales on their bodies and they breathe through their gills.

a   Write the letters A to E in your book.

b   Next to each letter, write the class of vertebrate that is described.

c   For each class, write two examples of animals that belong to it.

What did you learn?

1   What is the main difference between vertebrates and invertebrates?

2   List the five classes of vertebrates. Give one example in each class.

3   Parrots don't have teeth. How do they crack open the nuts and seeds that they want to eat?

4   Choose an animal you know well. Role-play how it finds and eats its food. Let your group guess which animal it is.

B Body parts for moving, hiding and protection

Explain

All animals have **external features**. These are the body parts on the outside of the body: beaks, claws, fur, ears and wings. Animals use their body parts to see and hear, to find food and eat it, to move from place to place and to protect themselves. Some features allow animals to be safe in their habitats.

Herons are birds that catch and eat fish, frogs and shellfish in shallow water. The diagram shows the external features of a heron and what the bird uses them for.

Science ideas

In this unit you will:

* describe some external body parts of different animals
* investigate how animals use different body parts to move, hide and protect themselves.

Key words

external features

Large eyes to spot prey

Strong spear-like beak for jabbing and catching fish, frogs and other prey

Long, flexible neck allows it to turn its head and to put its head into the water without its body getting wet

Mixed feather colours to blend into background when hunting and nesting

Large, strong wings for flying

Long, thin legs so body stays dry when standing in shallow water

Sharp claws for grip; claws are also used as a comb to clean feathers

Long, spread-out toes to help them walk in shallow water and on wet sand or mud without sinking in

Observe and infer

1   Read the information about the external features of reptiles.

Reptile bodies are covered with tough scales. Some reptiles have hard shells. The colour of the scales or the shells usually blends in with the colours of the habitat. Lizards and tortoises have legs and feet with claws, but snakes have no legs. Turtles have flippers with claws on the end to help them swim. Reptiles swim, run or slither to get away from danger. Reptiles usually have eyes on the sides of their head to help them spot predators and to find food.

a   Name the external features A to E. List them in your book.

b   Next to each feature, write its main function.

c   Tortoises live on land. They can pull all their body parts into their shells. How does this help them survive in their habitats?

2   Study the diagram and read the labels.

Eyes have a hard covering but no eyelids and are positioned so that fish can see all around it

Fins help the fish balance and move

Mouth for feeding

Gills are used for breathing under water

Overlapping tough scales protect the body

A strong tail acts like a fin

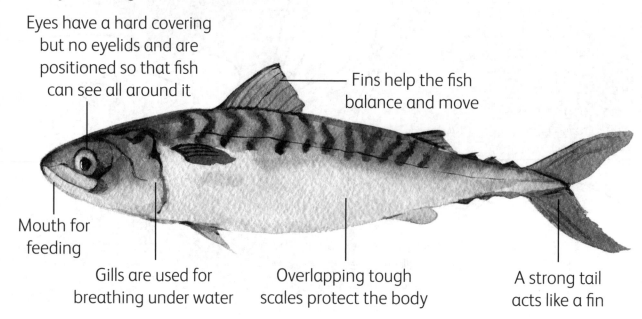

a Why do you think a fish needs so many fins?

b How does it help the fish to be able to see all around itself?

c Which features allow fish to swim close to rocks and other hard items in the water?

d What does a fish use its tail for?

Communicate

3 Do you know what all these animal parts are?
Read the words with a partner and discuss them. Then look up each word in a dictionary.

claws   paws   mouth   beak   teeth   shell   tongue
fins   wings   feet   eyes   nose   feathers   fur   hair   hands
horns   tusks   gills   hooves   tail   scales   fangs   whiskers   talons   skin

Design and make

Work in groups. You are going to make a set of picture dictionary cards to show what each word in the box means. Write each word on a card. Then draw or paste pictures to show what it means. Divide up the words so that everyone in your group makes some cards. Collect the materials you need for the task. Then make your set of cards.

Classify

4 Use the cards your group made in the previous activity.

a Sort the cards into groups to show what the different body parts are used for. Use these group headings:
   * Parts used to move from place to place
   * Parts used to protect itself or hide itself
   * Parts used for finding food or feeding

b Are there any parts that fit into more than one group? If so, decide which function is most important and put the part into that group.

Observe and record

5   Choose a mammal or an amphibian found in your country.

a   Draw the animal you have chosen and label the external features it uses to move.

b   List the ways in which the animal protects itself from danger.

Research and communicate

Some methods that animals use to protect themselves in their habitats are:

* mimicry: the animal tries to look or act like something else

* warning colours: bright or unnatural colours warn other animals that this animal might be poisonous or taste bad

* camouflage: the animal blends in with its surroundings so that it can't be easily seen.

6   For each method, find an example of an animal that protects itself in this way.

7   Make a fact file for each animal. Include a picture of each animal. Also include information about its external features.

What did you learn?

Copy this table into your book and complete it.

Class	Example of an animal in this class	Body part	Function
	Cat	Claws	
	Goat	Horns	
	Tortoise	Shell	
	Lizard	Legs	
	Eagle	Wings	
	Duck	Feet	
	Puffer fish	Spines	
	Grouper	Eye	

C Body parts for finding food and eating

Explain

Wild animals have to find their own food. Animals that eat other animals have to find them and catch them before they can eat them.

Chameleons are reptiles. They have long, sticky tongues that can shoot out quickly to catch insects. They also

A chameleon catching its prey

have eyes that can see in all directions. These features help them spot and catch their food.

* Animals eat different things and use different features to find, catch and eat food. Their features depend on what food they eat, but most animals find their food using their eyes, ears and noses.

* Amphibians and reptiles use their mouths to snap and grab food.

* Birds use their beaks and some use their talons to catch food and eat it. Birds have different types of beaks and talons that are suited to what they eat.

* Some fish use their mouths to scrape plants from rocks and eat them. Other fish are **predators**. They eat smaller **prey** animals, which they have to catch in their mouths.

* Mammals use their hands, paws and claws to hold or catch food. They use their teeth and mouth to tear and eat food. Different mammals have different teeth that are suited to the food they eat.

Science ideas

In this unit you will:

* describe some external body parts of different animals

* investigate how animals use different body parts to find food and eat it.

Key words

predator

prey

Observe and infer

1 Look at the pictures. Discuss what each animal eats.

a Choose one animal that eats seeds. Describe how it finds its food and eats it.

b Choose one animal that eats trees or grass. Describe how it eats.

c Choose one predator and explain how it catches and eats its food.

2 Cheetahs, owls and crocodiles are predators.

    a What does each animal eat?

    b How do they catch their prey?

3 Birds use their beaks to feed. The shape of a bird's beak can tell you what it eats.

    a Read this information about birds' beaks.

Beak type	Example	Food
Short and round		To catch insects and eat seeds
Long thin tube shape		For feeding on nectar from flowers
Sharp like a spear		For spearing fish and other small animals
Flat but pointed		To drill for insects and other invertebrates
Flat and slightly rounded		To strain algae or water weeds
Long and fat, shaped like a spoon		To scoop up fish and other small animals
Hooked, with a sharp end		To catch and tear smaller animals

b Describe the shape of each of the bird's beaks in photos A to K.

c Write the names of the birds in your book and use the shape of their beaks and what you already know about their beaks to work out what they eat.

A Heron

B Egret

C Flamingo

D Hawk

E Kingfisher

F Cuckoo

G Parrot

H Pigeon

I Martin

J Hummingbird

K Duck

Problem solving

4   Look at these objects and tools.

   a   Discuss how they work and what they are used for in everyday life.

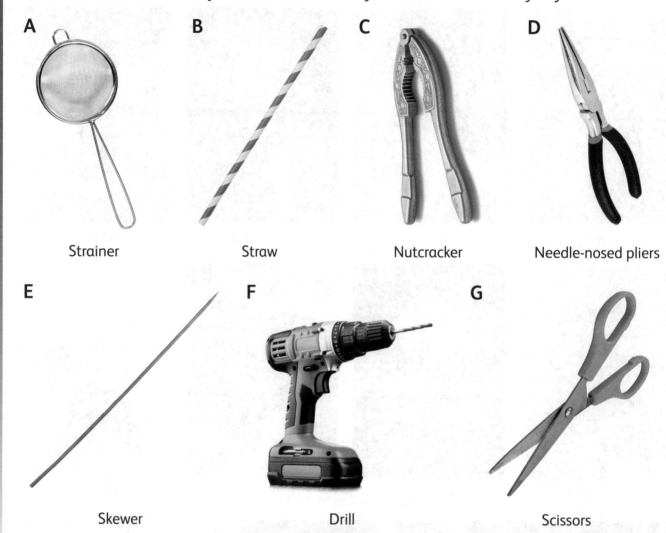

A   Strainer   B   Straw   C   Nutcracker   D   Needle-nosed pliers

E   Skewer   F   Drill   G   Scissors

   b   Birds use their beaks as tools to catch and eat food. Match each object or
        tool with a bird beak type. Explain your answers.

What did you learn?

Choose any two different types of vertebrates found in your environment.

1   Name each animal and sketch it to show its external features.
2   Write a sentence describing which body parts it uses for finding food and feeding.
3   Explain how it uses each body part to find food and eat it.

Topic 6 Review

Key ideas and concepts

Answer these questions about what you learnt in this topic.

1   What characteristic do all invertebrates share?

2   Draw five columns in your book and write the name of a
    vertebrate class at the top of each.

   a   Fill in the name of one animal in each class.

   b   Describe the animal's main external features.

   c   Write where each animal lives.

   d   Describe how each animal moves and stays safe in its habitat.

   e   List the parts the animal uses to find food and eat.

Think, talk, write …

1   Which class of vertebrates do you find the most in your country?
    Why do you think this is so?

2   Work in groups to design, draw and label an imaginary vertebrate.
    The animal you design must have these features:
   *   protective spikes
   *   colours that blend well with sand and rocks
   *   long, strong legs
   *   body parts that allow it to escape quickly
   *   features that allow it to eat both plants and meat.

Quick check

1   For each pair, list one difference in their external features.

   a   fish and amphibians

   b   fish and birds

   c   reptiles and birds

   d   birds and mammals

   e   fish and reptiles

   f   fish and mammals

   g   reptiles and mammals.

2   Write a sentence to describe how a gecko catches and eats its food.

Topic 7 Ecosystems

Teaching notes

Prior knowledge

* Students should know that food chains show feeding relationships among plants and animals, and habitats meet the needs of the living things within it. They should also understand the importance of caring for the environment and be able to identify some factors that harm it.

Food webs

* A food web shows how different food chains overlap and connect within a habitat. This allows us to see what eats what and to trace the energy flow from one organism to another.

* The Sun is the primary source of energy in all food webs. Green plants (producers) make their food from sunlight, air and water. Animals are consumers who get their energy from plants or other animals.

* Students will investigate factors that can disrupt food webs and how these factors affect the natural balance. Let them explore a local habitat and take note of the feeding relationships within it.

Ecosystems

* The living and non-living parts of an area form an ecosystem. Weather patterns, soils and land structure are examples of non-living parts.

* There are many different types of ecosystems in the Caribbean. Tropical rainforests, coral reefs, rocky shores and mangrove swamps are all examples of ecosystems.

* An ecosystem contains many habitats.

* Students will learn about different ecosystems and what makes them unique. They will also map the location of local ecosystems.

Recycling and conservation

* Conservation methods, including recycling, are important for maintaining or repairing our ecosystems.

* Students will study recycling within their school environment. They will also identify the negative outcomes that result from a lack of environmental protection.

What does this picture show? Who eats the seaweed? What does the shark eat? How do large fish get their energy? Why is sunlight important in food chains?

B

Look at this photograph carefully. Can you find the animal living there? Why do you think the animal has chosen to live there? Where would be a good place for a crab to live? Why? Would a city be a good place for a horse to live?

C

What can you see that is wrong in this picture? Would this be a good place for an animal to live? Which items are polluting the water? How did these items get into the water? How can we prevent water from getting polluted like this?

Think, talk and write

A **Food webs** *(pages 88–95)*

1 Work with a partner. Put each set of living things into a food chain with arrows to show who or what eats what.

Set A Crab Grouper Sea urchin Algae

Set B Snake Banana Mongoose Fruit bat

Set C Insect Pond weed Heron Toad

Set D Lion Acacia tree Zebra Hyena

2 Which animals are predators and which are prey in each food chain?

3 Choose an animal that lives in your area.

4 Where does the animal live?

5 What does it eat?

6 Does anything eat it? If so, what?

B **Ecosystems** *(pages 96–102)*

Work with a partner. Suggest one animal to replace the [?] in each food chain.

1 Leaves → Caterpillar → [?]

2 Seeds → Small bird → [?]

3 Leaf litter → Centipede → [?]

4 In which ways do animals need plants?

5 Why do plants need animals?

C **Recycling and conservation** *(pages 103–108)*

1 Draw a simple map of your school.

2 Mark all the places where you find waste or litter.

3 Use two different colours to show where recycling waste collections take place.

4 What can you do to improve waste management in your school?

A Food webs

Explain

A **food chain** is a diagram that shows where plants and animals get the food they need. All food chains depend on green plants, because plants use energy from the Sun to make their own food.

The arrows in a food chain show which way the energy is going. Here are three food chains:

Leaf $\longrightarrow$ Caterpillar $\longrightarrow$ Blue tit

Leaf $\longrightarrow$ Greenfly $\longrightarrow$ Ladybird

Leaf $\longrightarrow$ Caterpillar $\longrightarrow$ Blackbird

You can see that the leaf is part of all three food chains and that the caterpillar is in two. Food chains often overlap like this, so we put them together to form a **food web**.

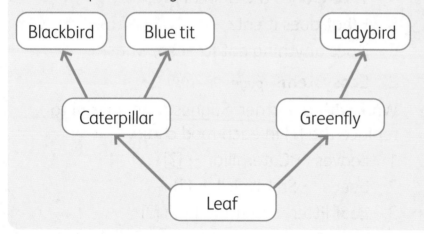

Science ideas

In this unit you will:

* learn how to draw and label food webs
* begin to understand how food webs are important for the balance of nature
* identify some of the things that may upset this balance
* study a local habitat.

Key words

food chain

food web

feeding relationships

balanced

balance of nature

Interpret and record

1   These food chains are found in the ocean.

Seaweed $\longrightarrow$ Giant clam $\longrightarrow$ Jellyfish

Seaweed $\longrightarrow$ Seahorse $\longrightarrow$ Sea snake

Seaweed $\longrightarrow$ Seahorse $\longrightarrow$ Jellyfish

Seaweed $\longrightarrow$ Shellfish $\longrightarrow$ Jellyfish

Food chains show us how animals and plants live together in ecosystems. It is important to care for our natural habitats and protect them from pollution.

Copy this food web into your book. Combine the food chains
to complete it. You may need to add missing arrows.

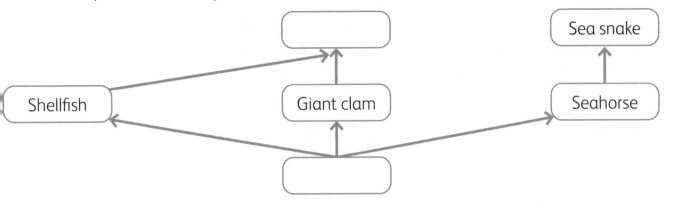

2 This food web shows the **feeding relationships** in a small pond. Study it
carefully and answer the questions.

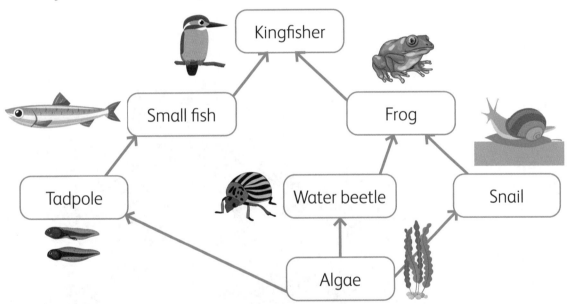

a What does the kingfisher eat?

b Which animals are eaten by the frog?

c From where does the small fish get its energy?

d What food provides energy for the snail?

e Name the plant that is providing food for the food web.

f From where does that plant get its energy?

g Describe how you know this is a food web and not a food chain.

h Draw a single food chain using the information in this food web.

Design and make

The design brief

You are going to work as a group to model a food web.
You will need: 20 pieces of string or wool, 10 cards for plant and animal names, a digital camera (or a phone with a camera).

Step 1: Prepare the cards

Write each of these words on a separate card.

Sun · green algae · seaweed · crab · flying fish

turtle · mahi mahi · pelican · shark

Step 2: Assign roles

* Choose nine students to sit in a circle. If you need space, you can do this outside.
* Pass the cards around so that each person in the circle gets one card.
* Choose a few students to use the string to make the connections to show the food web.
* Decide who will read out the instructions.
* You will also need one person to take a photo of your completed model.

Step 3: Make the model

Listen to these sentences. After each sentence is read out, make the feeding link using the string.

* The Sun provides energy for plants like seaweed and green algae.
* The flying fish eat green algae.
* The crab eats green algae.
* The flying fish eats seaweed.
* The flying fish eats the crab.
* The turtle eats the crab.
* The crab eats baby turtles.
* The mahi mahi eats the flying fish.
* The pelican eats the flying fish.
* The shark eats the mahi mahi.

Once you have made all the connections, take a photograph of your food web model before you break it up. If possible, print the photo for the classroom.

Step 4: Discuss the model

Answer these questions as a class.

* How did your model show feeding relationships?
* How is a model different from a food chain?

Step 5: Review

* Think about your model and then draw the food web you modelled. Use the feeding relationship sentences above to help you.
* Octopus eat mahi mahi and they may be eaten by sharks. Add an octopus to the food web you drew.

Interpret and record data

You will now think about the feeding relationships around you. Look at this picture of the plants and animals found in and around a small pond.

3   Answer these questions in your group.

   a   What plants can you see?

   b   Why are plants important in food webs?

   c   Ducks eat algae, plant leaves and roots, fish and fish eggs and snails. Where would be a good place for them in this pond?

   d   Why do you think is the heron standing in the water? What is it doing?

   e   Terrapins eat snails, small fish and water plants. Is this a good place for a terrapin to live? Why?

   f   Dragonflies eat insects like mosquitos. Why do you think they like to live near water?

   g   If you visit a pond like this one, you might not see all the animals that feed there. Explain why not.

4   Choose a small area in the school grounds. (Your teacher may give each group an area to study.)

   a   Observe the area you have chosen carefully. Identify as many plants and animals as possible. (You may need to gently lift stones or look under leaves for small creatures.) List them in your book.

b   Think about birds and other animals that might visit your area when you are not there. Add these to your list.

c   Remember to look for clues to see what the different animals eat.

To help us find out what is eating what we need to look for clues.

Clue 1: Where are the living things?

These termites are on a dead piece of wood because that is what they eat. Hummingbirds are often seen flying into flowers because that is what they eat.

Clue 2: Signs of feeding

This caterpillar eats leaves. You can see the holes in the leaves and you often find caterpillar droppings on the plants.

Smashed snail shells are a clue that a bird is eating the snails.

d   Discuss what you have found.

e   Work together to draw a food web that shows the feeding relationships for the area you observed. Work on a large sheet of paper and include drawings or photographs of the plants and animals.

f   Present your food web to the class and display it in the classroom so that other groups can look at it.

Food webs are balanced

A food web is **balanced** when all the living things within it have enough food and other things to live healthily.

Food webs change all the time. Animals are born. They grow, change and die. A tadpole will eat plants, but as a frog it will eat insects. In a pond, if there are fewer water beetles, frogs will eat more snails instead. These changes are natural and usually don't upset the balance.

The balance can be upset by larger events. If there is a drought, the pond might dry up, so plants and animals can no longer live there. People can also upset the balance of a food web by removing plants, dumping waste, catching and removing animals or causing a disturbance that scares animals away.

Balance is very important. Humans must look after this balance to make sure the plants and animals survive.

Predict and communicate

5   Look at the picture of the pond on page 92 again.

   a   What do you think would happen if the herons ate all the frogs and small fish in the pond? How would this affect the balance of the food web?

   b   What could cause all the tadpoles in the pond to die? How would this affect the balance of the food web?

6   This picture shows a grassland food web.

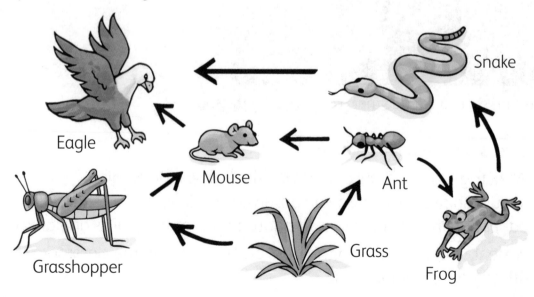

a Someone sets out poison that kills all the mice. Predict how this will affect the number of snakes.

b What will happen to the numbers of grasshoppers and ants if there are no mice left to eat them?

7 a Use this information about feeding relationships to draw a food web.

* An antelope eats grass.

* A zebra eats grass.

* A hyena eats zebra and antelope.

* A lion eats zebra, antelope and hyena.

b Write down one thing that might alter the **balance of nature** in this food web.

What did you learn?

1 Look at this food web carefully and answer the questions.

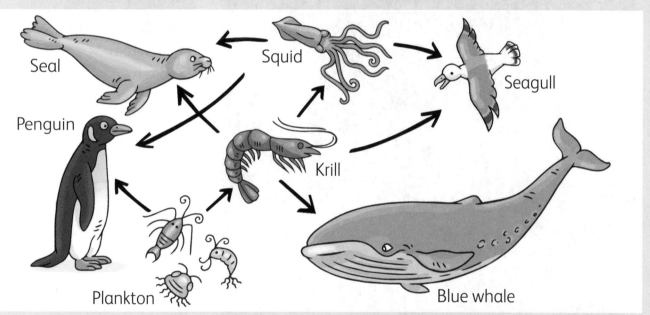

a Where would you find a food web like this one?

b What do penguins eat in this food web?

c Which animal eats penguins?

d If there is an oil spill and all the penguins are taken away to be cleaned, what will the seal have to eat?

e Why are the krill really important for the balance of this food web?

B Ecosystems

Explain

Everything around you is part of your environment. This includes living things such as plants, animals and people and non-living things such as rocks, water and soil.

An **ecosystem** is a community of living and non-living things that interact with each other in a particular area. Ecosystems are found on land, in rivers and ponds (fresh water) and in the sea (salt water).

There can be many different ecosystems in one country, and plants and animals live in different habitats within each ecosystem.

Science ideas

In this unit you will:

* learn what an ecosystem is
* find out about the different ecosystems in your country
* name the types of ecosystems in your country and show them on a map
* study a local ecosystem.

Key words

ecosystem

mangrove swamp

rainforest

coral reef

scrubland

marine

This photograph shows a **mangrove swamp**. This is one type of ecosystem found on islands in the Caribbean.

The picture shows some of the plants and animals that live in a mangrove swamp. Different animals live in different habitats in the mangrove ecosystem. The fish live in the water, and the egrets live in the trees.

Infer and predict

1   What are the three most important things that an animal or plant needs to get from an ecosystem to survive there?

2   Look at the mangrove swamp photo and picture.

   a   Mangrove swamps contain salt water. What does this tell you about where you might find them?

   b   Look at the birds that live in the mangroves. Where do they find their food?

   c   Farming and industry can cause mangrove swamps to dry up. How would this affect the balance in the ecosystem?

   d   Do you think you could find mangroves in high mountainous areas? Explain your answer.

3   Look carefully at this picture of a **rainforest** ecosystem.

a   Find these habitats in the picture and say what animals you
would expect to find in each:
   * a freshwater habitat
   * an underground habitat
   * a tree habitat.

b   Where would you expect these animals to live?
   * termites
   * iguanas
   * frogs

c   Describe the types of plants found in this ecosystem.

d   What type of weather conditions do you think you would
experience in a rainforest? Why?

Explain

The shape of the land, the weather conditions (temperature and rainfall) and the type of soil all affect what type of ecosystem you will find in an area. For example, rainforests are mainly found in hot areas, where it rains a lot all year round. In the Caribbean, **coral reefs** are found in warm seawater near the coast. Ocean ecosystems are found all over the world. The types of plants and animals found in each one depend on the temperature of the water. For example, penguins are only found in cold water ecosystems in the southern oceans, and polar bears are only found in the icy oceans near the North Pole.

Look at this map of an imaginary island. It shows the different types of ecosystems found in your region.

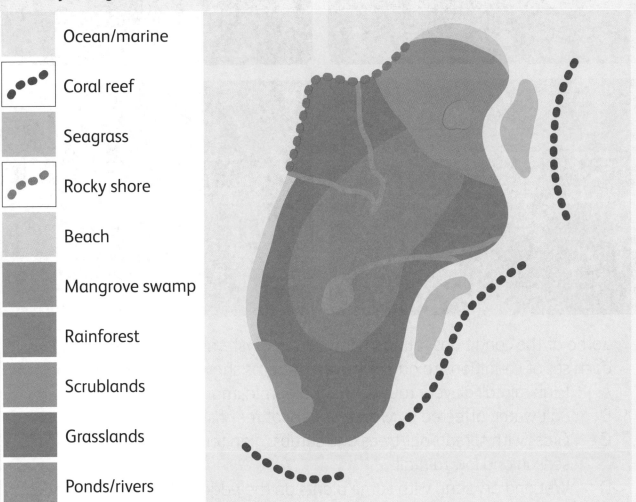

Ocean/marine

Coral reef

Seagrass

Rocky shore

Beach

Mangrove swamp

Rainforest

Scrublands

Grasslands

Ponds/rivers

✳ Ponds and rivers are freshwater ecosystems.

✳ The ocean, seagrass beds and coral reefs are salt water ecosystems.

✳ Rocky shores and beaches are coastal ecosystems. So are mangrove swamps.

✳ Grasslands, **scrublands** and rainforests are ecosystems found on land.

Interpret

4   Look at the photographs. List all the types of ecosystems you can find in each.

5   Some of the conditions found in different ecosystems are given here. Match each set of conditions to one of the ecosystems shown on the map on page 99.
   A   High rainfall all year round, hot and humid, many plants and trees
   B   Salt water, affected by waves, variety of reef fish
   C   Grass with spread-out trees and shrubs, high temperatures, a dry season and low rainfall
   D   Wet and dry sand with some plants on the edges, affected by the tides
   E   Muddy soil, salty water, affected by tides, plants have roots in the water
   F   Fresh running water, lots of rocks, some plants at the edges

6   Which of these ecosystems are found in your country? Tell your group which ones you have seen.

Investigate and record

You will now find out more about the ecosystems in your country.
Then you will show these on a map.

1   Draw a large outline map of your country on a sheet of paper.

2   Show the ocean ecosystems and draw in the main freshwater ecosystems.

3   Discuss the conditions needed for seagrass beds, coral reefs and mangrove swamps. If these are found in your country, mark them on the map.

4   Show the main beach ecosystems and any rocky shores (cliffs).

5   Think about the rainfall. Which parts of your country are dry, with grass and shrubs? Which parts are wetter with rainforests? Mark these on your map.

6   Label the different ecosystems on the map, or add a key to help others work out what your map shows.

Observe

7 Choose one ecosystem that can be found in your country.

   a List the non-living features of this ecosystem.

   b What types of plants are found there? Sketch the different kinds.

   c What animals live in this ecosystem? List as many as you can.

Communicate

8 The science advisor is coming to your school. Prepare a report on your chosen ecosystem to present. Include photographs, drawings and maps in your report.

What did you learn?
Bequia is an island of St Vincent and the Grenadines. The photograph shows Bay Beach on Bequia.

1 What **marine** ecosystems would you expect to find on Bequia? Find evidence of these in the photograph.

2 Sea turtles feed on seagrass and lay their eggs on sandy beaches. Would this be a good habitat for them? Why?

3 Bequia has very little rainfall and there are no permanent streams or rivers on the island. Use this information to work out which two ecosystems would not be found there.

4 A bird watcher listed some of the birds she saw in one ecosystem on Bequia. What type of ecosystem do you think it was? Why?

> Brown pelicans
> Belted kingfisher
> Mangrove cuckoo
> Purple-necked heron

5 The main land ecosystem on Bequia is scrubland. What does this mean?

C Recycling and conservation

Explain

Many materials we use daily are made from **natural resources**. Think about paper, for example. The diagram below shows which natural resources we use to make paper.

Natural resources can be damaged or used up. For example, if we cut down too many trees, wood will become scarce. If we pollute our water resources, they will be damaged and we cannot use them. Protecting and saving our natural resources is called **conservation**.

Many materials and products are thrown away as waste after use. This waste pollutes the environment. **Recycling** can help protect the environment and can help conserve resources. Recycling involves finding new uses for waste items.

Some items take hundreds of years to break down naturally. That is why it is important to remove them from our environment as much as possible.

Science ideas

In this unit you will:

* learn about recycling and how it can help keep the balance in nature
* understand how conservation methods protect the environment
* explain why we need conservation
* investigate what might happen if we don't protect our environment.

Key words

natural resources
conservation
recycling   overfishing

Natural resources used to make paper

Wood from trees   Fresh water   Energy from the Sun   Paper

Discuss and hypothesise

1   This poster shows some items you can recycle. In some countries, some types of waste are burned to make electricity. Discuss the poster in your groups.

2 **a** Which of these items can be recycled?

b List three classroom garbage items that can be recycled.

c Plant waste (peels, cores and rotten fruit) cannot be recycled. What can you do with it to make sure it is not wasted?

3 Look at this sign in a shop window.

a Why is this store trying to convince shoppers to bring and use their own reusable shopping bags?

b Reusable shopping bags are often made from recycled plastic materials. How does this help the environment?

> **1 Reusable bag replaces:**
> - **6 plastic bags per week**
> - **24 plastic bags per month**
> - **288 plastic bags per year**
> - **22 176 plastic bags in an average lifetime**

4 Write down one way in which you could:

a reduce the number of plastic bags you use

b reuse plastic shopping bags for other things

c recycle plastic bags.

Design and construct

The design brief
Collect some recyclable items from home or at school that you can use to make a musical instrument.
You will need: recyclable items, glue, string.

Step 1: Think and plan
Look at the materials you collected. Decide what sort of instrument you are going to make. Will it be something to blow, bang or strum?

Step 2: Test
Use your instrument with your group to make some musical sounds.

Infer and communicate

5　Look at the picture carefully.

    a　Why are these farmers collecting rain water?

    b　How does this help to conserve the environment?

    c　Make a list of ways in which you could conserve water at school.

    d　Why is it important to conserve fresh water supplies?

Interpret

6　This map shows an area of St Lucia where the sea area along the coast is being used for different activities.

This map shows an area of St Lucia where the sea area along the coast is being used for different activities.

The bright green areas are marine reserves. These reserves have strict rules and are especially important for the conservation of marine ecosystems. Fishing in marine reserves is prohibited, or limited to certain types of fish. This is to stop **overfishing** and to protect threatened species of fish such as blue fin tuna.

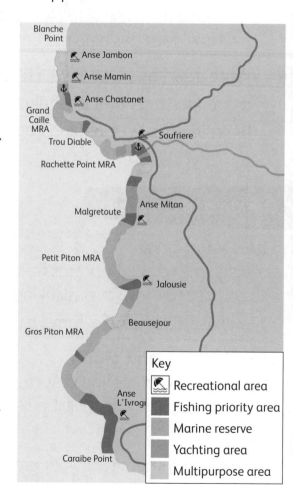

    a　Discuss with your group what is meant by overfishing.

    b　Write down three ways in which overfishing affects the marine ecosystem.

    c　How will stopping the fishermen going into this area help conserve the ecosystem?

Observe and infer

7   Look at the rubbish this street market has produced.

a   What types of rubbish can you see in the picture?

b   Which types of rubbish will affect your environment most?

c   Some students decide to clear all the plastic waste, clean it and use it to make other things. These are some of the things they made:

Think of two other things you could make from cleaned plastic.

d   Reusing plastic rubbish removes the plastic waste already in the environment. But can we reduce the amount of plastic being dumped in the first place? Write down some ideas for reducing plastic waste.

e   This sculpture is made entirely of plastic taken from the ocean. Would this statue make people in your community and tourists think about their plastic waste?

Design and make

The design brief

You know that it is important to look after your environment. Work with a partner to design a poster to show what could happen if we *don't* look after our environment. Include text, photos and captions.

Step 1: Think and plan

* What will your poster look like?
* What information do you want to include?
* What drawings or photos do you want to show?

Step 2: Make a rough sketch

Sketch a rough design to decide how to set out your poster.

Step 3: Create your poster

Use your rough sketch to create your poster. Make sure it includes text, photos or drawings, and captions.

Step 4: Explain

Use your poster to explain to another group why it is important to look after your environment.

What did you learn?

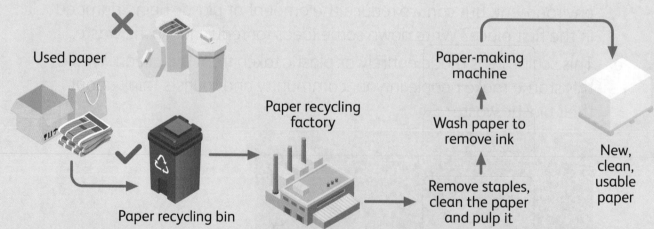

Used paper

Paper recycling bin

Paper recycling factory

Remove staples, clean the paper and pulp it

Wash paper to remove ink

Paper-making machine

New, clean, usable paper

1   What natural resources are you saving if you recycle used paper?

2   Write down three ways in which you could reuse a cardboard box.

Topic 7 Review

Key ideas and concepts

A new student has arrived in your class and wants to know what you have been learning. Use these headings. Write a short summary to show what you have learnt. Give an example of each to help them understand what you have learnt.

| Food webs | Ecosystems | Recycling |

Think, talk, write ...

1 Make up a song or rap to encourage people to recycle.

2 With a partner, write down ten quiz questions about food webs, ecosystems, recycling and conservation. Ask another pair your quiz questions.

Quick check

1 What is the difference between a food chain and a food web?

2 Copy these sentences. Then choose words from the box to complete the sentences.

> recycling   rain   litter   chemicals   natural
> air   waste   conserves   energy   swamps

a The major source of _____ in a food web is the Sun.

b Producers make their own energy using sunlight, _____ and water.

c The balance of food webs can be upset by _____ or human-made events.

d Examples of natural events might be lack of _____ or an animal disease.

e Humans alter the natural balance in many ways. _____ used by farmers, poisonous substances from factories or dumping of _____ materials will upset this balance.

f Rainforests, grasslands and _____ are examples of Caribbean ecosystems.

g At home you can help conserve your environment by putting _____ in a waste bin, saving water and _____ or reusing.

h Recycling is important, because it _____ natural resources.

Teaching notes

Prior knowledge

✱ Students should know about energy and how different types of energy affect the lives of people (for example, energy from food, and electrical energy).

✱ They should already have experimented with devices that use moving air or water as sources of energy, such as windmills and water wheels. They also know about food chains and how energy flows in ecosystems.

Light and heat

✱ The Sun is the main provider of heat and light on Earth. People use energy from heat and light for different purposes every day.

✱ Both heat and light are forms of energy.

✱ Other objects also emit light, such as candles and fire. Many objects that give off light also give off heat. When this heat is not used, we call this wasted heat. For example, a light bulb gives off heat that is wasted.

Fuels and their uses

✱ Fuel is any substance that we burn to produce energy. The most common fuels are oil, gasoline (petrol), diesel, kerosene, liquid petroleum gas, wood, charcoal and coal.

✱ When fuels burn, they produce smoke and other chemicals that enter the atmosphere and cause pollution.

Energy transformations

✱ Energy is never used up or destroyed. It constantly cycles and transforms from one type to another.

✱ Students should know that animals get energy from eating plants and plants get energy from sunlight. As they know that plants change sunlight into food (energy), use this to introduce the concept of energy transformation.

✱ At this level, students need to describe the transformations. For example, a toaster transforms electrical energy into heat energy, and a coalpot transforms stored energy in wood or coal into heat energy that is used to cook food.

A

Have a look at the photo of the Sun and the plants. What is their relationship with each other? In this system, which is the input and which is the output?

B

Why do you think there is smoke coming out of the chimneys? Can you guess what type of fuel is creating the smoke? Do you think the smoke is good or bad? Why?

C

What does this image show? How do all the plants and animals interact? How does the Sun fit into this system?

Think, talk and write

A Light and heat *(pages 112–117)*

1 We get light from the Sun. Can you think of some other ways in which sunlight is important to us?

2 What do you think would happen if there was no sunlight? Discuss this with a partner.

B Fuels and their uses *(pages 118–119)*

Unscramble these words to find four types of fuel we use in everyday life.

1 loi   2 nesekreo

3 trolep   4 olaccarh

Complete these sentences.

5 Gasoline is used as a fuel in _____ and _____.

6 Diesel is used as a fuel in _____ and _____.

7 We use wood as a fuel to _____, _____ and _____.

8 What is your body's source of fuel?

C Energy transformations *(pages 120–122)*

1 What is happening in this picture?

2 Where did the door get the energy from to move?

3 What other objects in this image have energy? Where do they get it from?

A Light and heat

Explain

The **Sun** is the main source of light and heat on Earth. Both light and heat are forms of energy, and energy from the Sun is called **solar energy**. Without solar energy the Earth would be a very cold and dark place, and no animals or plants would be able to survive.

We need **light** to see all the things around us. This diagram shows some of the **natural sources** of light and artificial objects (made by people) that produce or emit (give out) light.

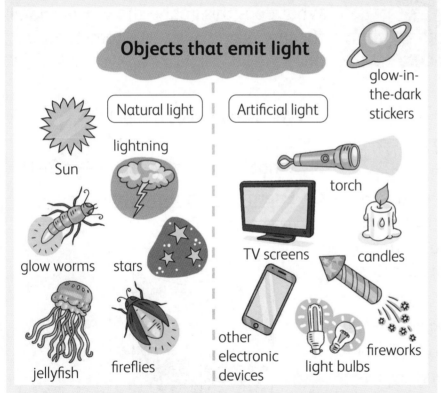

Objects that emit light

glow-in-the-dark stickers

Natural light | Artificial light

Sun

lightning

torch

TV screens

candles

glow worms | stars

other electronic devices

light bulbs

fireworks

jellyfish | fireflies

Artificial sources of light allow us to see in the dark, to watch TV and to work in dark places like caves and mines.

A

B

Science ideas

In this unit you will:

* identify different objects that give off light
* explain how the Sun gives us light and heat on Earth
* describe how we use this heat and light in everyday activities.

Key words

Sun
solar energy
light
natural sources
artificial sources

Many objects that emit light also produce heat. Lamps get hot when they have been on for a while. Burning objects also give off heat. Our bodies produce heat too.

Heat energy is very useful. We use heat to cook food, to boil water, to dry our clothes, to iron and to warm up cold spaces.

Safety note

Heat can be dangerous. Always be careful when you use heat sources to avoid burning yourself.

Infer and predict

1   Look at the pictures.

a   What is happening in each picture?

b   What time of day are these activities taking place? How can you tell?

c   Is it possible to do these activities at night? Explain.

Observe and record

2   You are going to identify objects that emit light at school or at home.

a   Draw up a table like this one in your book.

Object	Natural	Artificial	Gives off heat

b   List the objects you can find that emit light.

c   Tick the correct column to show whether each object is natural or artificial and whether or not it also gives off heat.

Communicate

3   How do you use energy from the Sun in your home? Discuss this with a partner. Write down your ideas.

Interpret

4   Read this information about some of the ways in which we use solar energy.

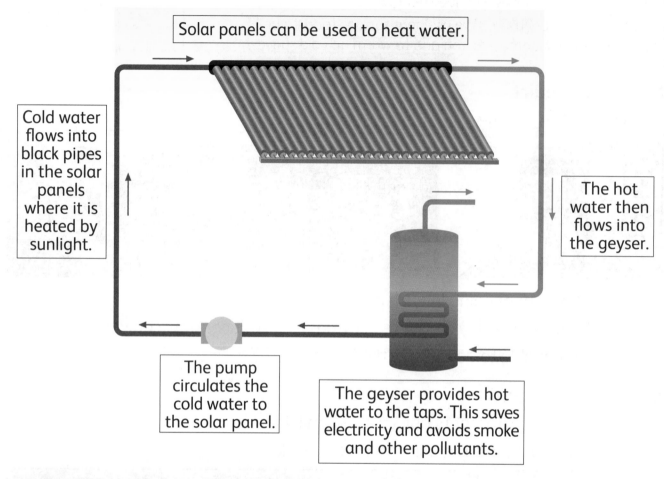

Solar panels can be used to heat water.

Cold water flows into black pipes in the solar panels where it is heated by sunlight.

The hot water then flows into the geyser.

The pump circulates the cold water to the solar panel.

The geyser provides hot water to the taps. This saves electricity and avoids smoke and other pollutants.

Solar cookers focus sunlight and trap heat. Water can reach boiling point in solar cookers. This type of stove is common in our region and solar cookers are also useful on yachts.

This is a solar charging station for electronics. The panels convert sunlight to electricity, which is stored in special batteries in the unit. You can plug phones and other electronics into the unit to charge them.

Now answer these questions about solar energy.

a   How do solar panels on a roof heat water for use in the home?

b   What is the advantage of using a solar cooker?

c   Why do you think solar cookers are popular with sailors?

d   When is a solar charging unit useful? Why?

e   Why is the Caribbean a good place to use solar energy for heating water, for cooking and for charging devices?

Investigate

Do you think the colour of a container makes a difference to the time it takes to heat up the water inside it?

You will need: three empty plastic bottles (the same size), black and white paint, a thermometer, a clock, water.

1   Plan a fair test to answer these questions.

Question A: Does water heat up faster if the container is painted a darker colour?

Question B: Does the water get hotter if the container is painted a darker colour?

2   Write a hypothesis (in your hypothesis you say what you think will happen).

3   Answer these questions before you start.

a   What will we keep the same to make sure our test is fair?

b   What is the one thing we will change?

c   What will we measure?

4   Carry out your investigation. Use a table to record your results.

5   Answer these questions based on what you found out.

a   Which colour container heated water faster?

b   Which colour container's water was hotter at the given time?

c   If you wanted to heat water using solar energy, what colour pipes and containers would you use? Why?

Observe and infer

5   Here are some devices you may have in your home.

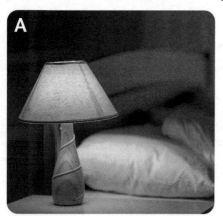

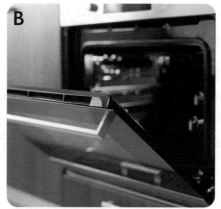

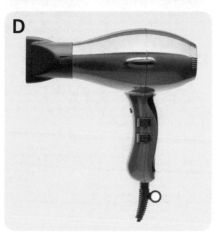

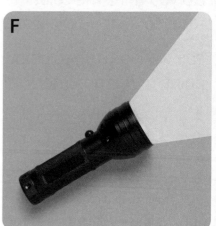

a   Write the name of each device and for what you would use it.

b   All these devices produce heat. Which devices produce heat that is not used in any way (wasted heat)?

6   Animals (including humans) also produce heat.

a   Do you know your body temperature? Use a thermometer to find out what it is.

b   What is the temperature outside? Have a look at the weather report in the newspaper or online to find this out.

c   What can you do to cool down when the temperature is very hot and you feel uncomfortable?

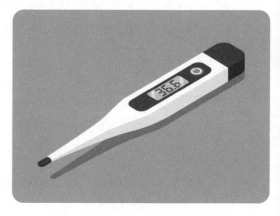

Investigate

You know that there are natural and artificial (human-made) objects that produce heat. Let's look at how different our lives would be if we did not have these objects! Get into small groups and choose one object from the pictures.

In your groups, find information about your object:

* When was the device invented?
* Who invented it?
* How does the device work?
* How does the device make it convenient and safe for people to use the heat it produces in their homes?
* What would your life be like without this device?
* Could you use a different device for the same purpose?

What did you learn?

1 Give one example of a human-made and one example of a natural object that produces light.

2 Write down three objects at school or at home that produce both light and heat. Is the heat from these devices used?

3 Do you think it is possible to use solar energy at night?

B Fuels and their uses

Fuels are substances or materials that can be burned to produce energy. The fuel for this coalpot is **charcoal**.

Much of the energy we use comes from **fossil fuels**, such as coal, **natural gas** and **oil**. Gasoline and diesel (made from oil) provide energy for cars and other vehicles to make them move.

The process of gathering these fuels can harm the environment. When we burn these fuels, they release **pollutants** into the air.

Solar energy is a **renewable resource**. So is wind energy. Some people use solar panels on their homes to convert sunlight into electricity. Wind energy is used to turn wind generators and produce electricity.

Solar and wind energy are far less damaging to the environment than fossil fuels because they don't give off pollutants.

Science ideas

In this unit you will:
* find some examples of fuels used in your home, for transport and to make things
* identify and discuss some of the consequences of using fuels in different ways.

Key words

fuels	oil
charcoal	pollutants
fossil fuels	renewable
natural gas	resource

Infer

1   Jack's mom says that her car is empty and she needs to fill it up.

   a   What do you think Jack's mom means?

   b   With what will she fill the car up?

   c   Where will Jack's mom go to fill up her car?

2   Look at the pictures.

a   What type of fuel is being used in each picture?

b   What is it being used for?

c   Is any pollution being produced by burning the fuel?

Classify and record

3   Identify machines or equipment in your home or your community that use gasoline, diesel, kerosene, wood, coal or gas as a source of fuel. Record your findings in a table.

Communicate

4   Look at the picture of traffic on a busy road.

a   Why is there so much smoke in the picture?

b   What effect do you think this smoke will have on people?

c   Do you think the smoke will affect plants and animals? Why?

d   Can you think of ways to reduce the pollution from the cars?

5   Saving energy helps cut down on pollution and makes non-renewable energy sources last longer. Make a list of energy saving actions that you can take to reduce the amount of energy used in your home and at school.

What did you learn?

1   What is the difference between a renewable and a non-renewable energy source?

2   Why is it important to know about the negative effects of fuels on the environment?

C Energy transformations

Explain

All living things get **energy** from food. Plants use light energy from the Sun to make their own food. Animals cannot make their own food, so they eat plants or other animals to get their energy.

The picture shows how energy is passed along in an **ecosystem**.

* Plants get energy from the Sun. They change it into food.
* Cows get energy from the plants they eat. They use this energy to grow and produce milk.
* People get energy when they drink milk or eat plants or meat.

Science ideas

In this unit you will:

* trace the flow and exchange of energy in an ecosystem
* understand examples of how energy is transformed.

Key words

energy
ecosystem
transformed
transformation

We can draw a food chain to show this flow of energy. Remember that the arrows show the direction in which energy is flowing.

Sun → Grass → Cow → People

Energy can be changed or **transformed** from one form to another.

* Solar energy is transformed by plants into food energy.
* Energy from food is transformed to movement energy when you run.
* Energy stored in coal is transformed into heat energy when coal burns.
* Energy from a battery is transformed into electrical energy and then into light energy when a flashlight is switched on.

We can draw flow diagrams to show energy **transformations**. For example:

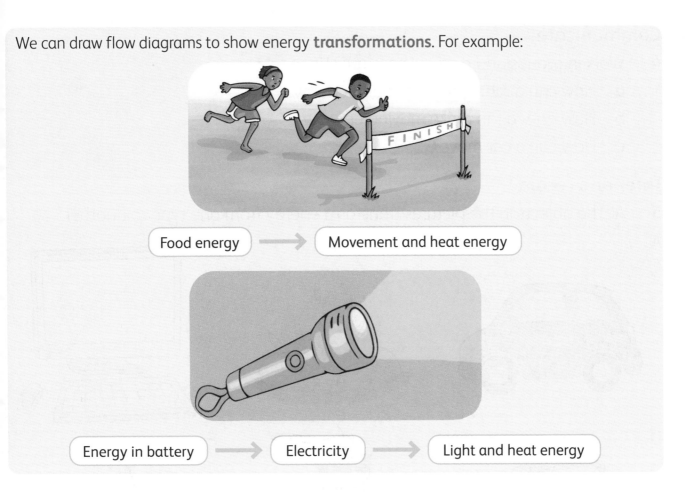

Food energy ⟶ Movement and heat energy

Energy in battery ⟶ Electricity ⟶ Light and heat energy

Infer and communicate

1 What do you think will happen to plants if they don't get any sunlight? Give a reason for your answer.

2 Look at the photograph.

a What are the giraffe doing in this picture?

b Why do the giraffe need to eat?

c What do the giraffe get from the food? Why is this important?

d Draw a simple food chain to show how energy flows from the Sun to the giraffe.

3 Draw food chains for two things that you eat that give your body energy. Start each food chain with the Sun.

121

Communicate

4 Work in groups and discuss these questions.

    a How can a radio produce sound energy?

    b How does a fan make moving energy?

    c How can a car move?

Infer and record

5 All the objects in the pictures transform energy from one type to another.

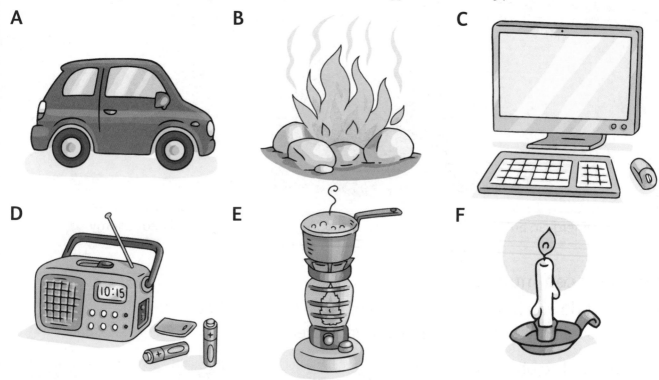

A   B   C

D   E   F

    a Write down the names of all the objects in the pictures.

    b Next to each name, write the source of its energy.

    c Draw flow diagrams to show how energy is transformed in each item.

What did you learn?

1 Where does your body get its energy from?

2 Write down three things that use energy from batteries. Draw a flow diagram for each one to show how it transforms energy from the battery into other forms of energy.

Topic 8 Review

Key ideas and concepts

One of your classmates missed this topic at school. Use these headings
to summarise what you learnt in this topic.

* Solar energy   * Fuels

* Pollution   * Energy flows in ecosystems

* Energy transformations

Think, talk, write …

1   Do we use more energy when it is hot or when it is cool? Why do you say so?

2   What alternatives do you think can best replace non-renewable
    fuels (for example, coal and petroleum)? Do you think it is possible
    for everyone to change to these alternatives?

3   Where do you think the best place would be to put a wind generator
    in your community? Why?

Quick check

1   Answer these questions in your book.

    a   What is the Earth's main source of heat and light?

    b   What do we call the instrument we use to measure heat?

    c   What kind of energy makes things get warmer?

    d   What kind of energy do we use to see things when it is dark?

    e   Name two sources of heat in your home.

    f   Name two sources of light that don't need electricity.

    g   Name one item at home that gives off both heat and light.

2   What type of fuel is used in these machines?

    a   stove   b   aeroplane

3   Draw flow diagrams to show how energy is transformed when:

    a   you boil water in a kettle   b   you cook food on a gas stove.

4   Draw a comic to show what might happen if there was no light or
    no heat for a day.

Forces, motion and structure

Teaching notes

Prior knowledge

* Students should know that a force can stop or start movement and cause an object to speed up or slow down when it is already moving. They should also remember how to classify structures in different ways, and know about different mechanical devices.

Pushing and pulling forces

* Students should remember that motion can be changed. They will now identify the forces that cause these changes.

* When you teach this topic, it is helpful to show students examples of forces at work in everyday situations. For example, we push a switch to turn on the light, or we push a ball with a bat to change its direction.

Magnets

* Magnets exert a force over a distance. This can cause magnetic materials to move.

* Magnetic force attracts or pulls magnetic materials towards the magnet.

Structures

* The strength of a material determines how much load it can take before bending or breaking. Different structures can be strengthened by folding, reinforcing, filling or increasing the thickness of materials.

* Students learn about human-made structures and investigate what makes these strong.

* Stems of plants keep them upright. Students study the cross-section of a tree trunk to learn more about its structure.

* In Topic 6, students learnt about vertebrates and their internal skeletons. In this topic they learn about exoskeletons and how these protect animals that do not have an internal skeleton.

A

What happens in this photo? Is the boy pushing or pulling the swing? How did you decide?

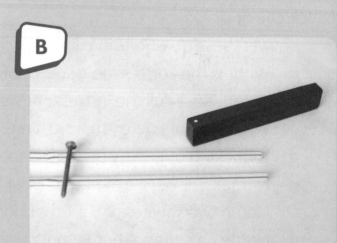

B

Troy has set up this equipment. He says he can make the nail roll without touching it. What equipment has he used? What are the straws for? What will he use the magnet for? Do you think he can make the nail move without touching it?

Crabs are not vertebrates, so they do not have bones inside their bodies. What do crabs have instead of bones? How does this help them move? Describe what you think the crab's skeleton is like.

Think, talk and write

A Pushing and pulling forces
(pages 126–129)

Work in pairs. Take turns to show how you would use a broom to sweep the floor.

1 Do you push or pull the broom as you sweep? Explain your answer.

2 Think of other examples where you use pushing or pulling to make things move. Share your ideas with the class.

B Magnets (pages 130–132)

1 Have you used a magnet before? What did you use it for?

2 How do you think a magnet works? Draw and label a picture to show your ideas.

C Structures (pages 133–138)

Imagine you have to build a bridge to get across a gulley.

1 What materials would you use? Why?

2 How would you make sure the bridge was strong enough for a person to cross it?

3 Kyle has these three cups.

paper   pastic   styrofoam

Which cup do you think could support the heaviest rock?

4 How would you test whether your prediction was correct?

5 How would you make sure that your test was fair?

A Pushing and pulling forces

Explain

You can move things by pushing or pulling them. When you **push** or **pull** something you are using **force**.

A

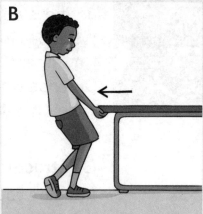

B

Pushing force   Pulling force

A pulling force makes things move towards your body.
A pushing force moves things away from your body.

You cannot see forces, but you can see the effect they have on objects. Forces can make objects move or stop moving. Forces can make objects go faster or slower. Forces can also make something change direction.

Pushing or pulling objects can make them change shape by squashing or stretching them.

A

B

You can squash a ball of Plasticine   You can stretch an elastic band

Science ideas

In this unit you will:
* describe and show pushing and pulling forces
* give examples to show how we use forces at home and in our daily lives.

Key words

push
pull
force

Observe and infer

1   Look at the different actions below.

> dragging a chair   rowing a boat   pressing the button in a lift
> typing on a keyboard   brushing your hair

a   Which actions are pushing actions?

b   Which actions are pulling actions?

c   Are any actions both pushing and pulling actions?

2   Make a list of ten pushing or pulling actions that you do daily.

Communicate

3   Work with a partner.

a   Describe what is happening in each picture.

b   Identify the type of force (or forces) that are at work in each example.

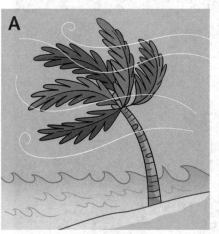

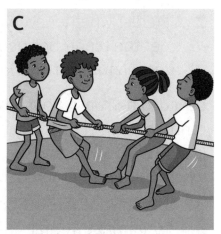

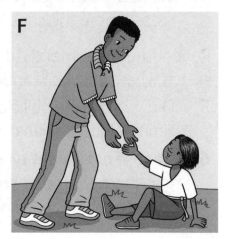

Investigate and record

How much force is needed to move a tennis ball? Work in groups of three to investigate this.

You will need: a tennis ball, a grassy area, a cone to mark a position on the grass, string or tape to make lines on the field.

What you need to do:
* Use tape to make a line on the grass. This is where you will stand.
* Place the cone at least five paces from the line.
* Roll the tennis ball along the grass, trying to get it to the cone.
* Each person in your team will take a turn.

Answer these questions before your start:
1   What forces will act on the tennis ball when you roll it across the grass?
2   Predict whether everyone in your group will get the tennis ball near the cone. Give a reason for your answer.

Let each person in your team take a turn to roll the tennis ball towards the cone. Then draw a rough sketch of the field and the cone and make a mark where each team member's ball stopped.
3   Did anyone get the ball to stop at the cone?
4   What does this tell you about forces if the ball stops before the cone?

Repeat the experiment. Add another mark on your sketch where your ball landed.
5   Did you get the ball closer to the cone this time? What did you do differently?
6   Choose a different type of ball and investigate whether you need more or less force to roll it to the cone. Try to explain why.

Classify

4   Study the picture carefully.

a   How many examples of pulling forces can you find?
    Show them to your partner.

b   How many examples of pushing forces can you find?
    Show them to your partner.

What did you learn?

1   Read each statement. Write down whether it is true or false.
    a   Forces can be seen.
    b   The effects of a force can be seen and felt.
    c   A push is a force that brings an object closer to us.
    d   To move an object, you have to apply a force.
    e   A force can change an object's speed.
    f   A force cannot change an object's size.

2   Draw and label sketches to show the forces at work when you:
    a   get out of bed
    b   write in your book
    c   play tennis.

B Magnets

Explain

A **magnet** is a special type of metal which can **attract** (pull) some types of metals towards it.

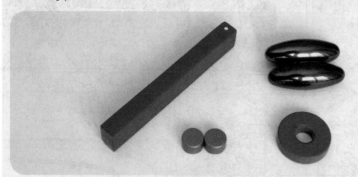

Materials that are attracted to a magnet are called magnetic materials.

Magnets can **repel** (push away) other magnets.

When you exert a pushing or a pulling force with your body, you need to touch the object you are pushing or pulling. Magnets can exert a force to push or pull objects that are some distance away from them. Magnets can also exert a force through some other materials.

Science ideas

In this unit you will:

* investigate how magnets can make different materials move.

Key words

magnets
attract
repel

Predict and record

1   Predict which of these objects will be attracted to a magnet. Write the words in your book.

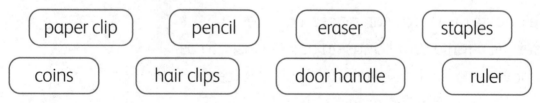

paper clip   pencil   eraser   staples

coins   hair clips   door handle   ruler

2   Test your predictions by placing a magnet close to each object.

3   Were your predictions correct?

4   One student found that her hair clip and ruler were magnetic. Another student found that hers were not. Write a sentence to explain why both students could be correct.

Investigate and record

From how far away can a magnet pull an object? To find this out, do this investigation with a partner.

You will need: a sheet of paper, a plastic or wooden ruler, a pencil, a magnet and a small magnetic object (staples, paper clips and drawing pins will work).

Set up your equipment as shown.

Use the pencil to slowly push the object closer and closer to the magnet until the magnet pulls it. Mark and record the distance from where it is pulled by the magnet.

Then answer these questions in your book.

1   Why do you need to use a plastic or wooden ruler?

2   What happened when the object got close enough to feel the magnet's force?

3   Investigate and report what happens if:
    a   you use a smaller or bigger object
    b   you stick two magnets together.

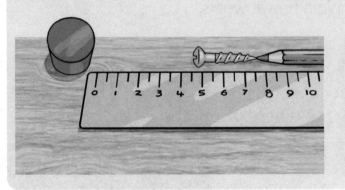
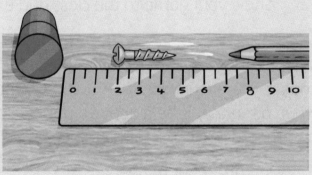

Design and make

Games and toys that use magnets and movement

Work in groups to design and make your own simple toy or game that uses magnets to make things move.

1 Look at these games and toys. Discuss how they work.

Magnetic maze

Magnetic slime

How-many-can-you-grab game

Fishing game

Bottle top magnet families

2 Show your game to the class and explain how it works.

What did you learn?

Look at the picture carefully. It shows what happens when a magnet is held above a paper clip that is tied to a thread and stuck to the table.

1 Describe what happens.

2 Explain why this happens.

3 What do you think will happen if the magnet is taken away? Why?

C Structures

Explain

A **structure** is something made of different parts. The **material** we use and how we put the parts together can make the structure strong or weak. The strength of a structure determines how big or heavy a load it can hold without bending or breaking.

Science ideas

In this unit you will:

* find out how people can make structures stronger
* observe tree trunks to find out how natural structures are built up over time
* investigate and classify animals based on the type of skeleton they have.

Key words

structure
material
reinforce
folding
natural
cross-section
endoskeleton
exoskeleton

There are different ways to make the materials that we use for building structures stronger:

* we can **reinforce** the material by making it thicker – by using cardboard instead of paper
* we can arrange blocks in rows or layers and fill them to strengthen them further
* **folding** can also strengthen materials by making them thicker or by changing their shape
* thin items like small twigs and branches can be tied to thicker items to make them stronger.

Communicate

1   Think about a time when you had to make something that you built stronger. Discuss these questions in your group.

   a   Why did you need to make the structure stronger?

   b   How did you make it stronger?

   c   Was it easy or challenging? Why?

   d   Did your ideas work? Explain why or why not.

2   Look at this photograph carefully.

Reinforced concrete pillars

   a   What is the construction company doing to strengthen the concrete pillars?

   b   Why do you think concrete in buildings needs to be strong?

   c   What could happen if the pillars holding up a bridge are not reinforced or strengthened in any way?

Design

Design different ways to strengthen paper

Investigate different ways to use a single sheet of paper to support the mass of your ruler.

You will need: at least five sheets of paper, sticky tape, your ruler.

1   Look at the pictures below for some ideas to strengthen paper.

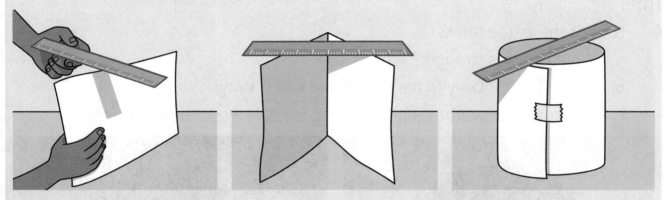

2   Can you balance a ruler on one sheet of A4 paper? How?

3   Aliyah folded her paper like this:

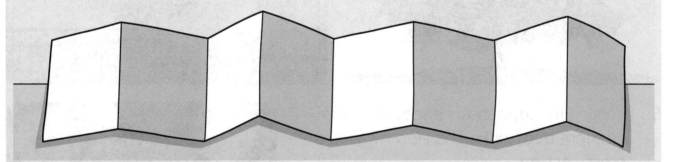

How does this help her make the paper stronger?

4   Can you find any examples of this way of making materials stronger in real life?

Observe

3   Find different structures around your school. Go for a walk outside and make a note of all the structures you see.

   a   Discuss your list of structures in a group. How many structures did you find?

   b   How do these structures support a load and forces so that they do not break?

Natural structures

Explain

Trees are strong **natural** structures. Tree roots go deep into the ground to support the tree's trunk and branches and to keep it anchored. Tree trunks have many layers of wood inside them. These layers help to make the trunk strong.

Infer

4   Look at these tree trunks.

   a Which trunk is stronger? Why?

   b Which trunk is likely to bend in strong wind? Why?

   c Gardeners sometimes support young trees. How do they do this?

A

B

5   This photograph shows a special view of different tree trunks. This view is called a **cross-section**.

   a Draw a tree. Then draw a line where you think the tree was cut so we can see this view.

   b Why do you think there are circular lines on the inside of the tree trunks?

   c Compare the cross-sections of the different tree trunks. What do they tell you about the trees that were cut down?

What is an exoskeleton?

Explain

You already know that vertebrates have skeletons inside their bodies. When the skeleton is inside a body it is called an **endoskeleton**.

Many animals don't have bones at all. Some animals, like crabs and beetles, have a stiff covering, called an **exoskeleton**, on the outside of their bodies.

Exoskeletons can be stiff, leathery or made from shell. Their functions are to give the body shape, to protect the soft internal organs and to help the animal move.

Some animals that have an exoskeleton are spiders, shrimps and scallops.

A

spider:
tough and leathery

B
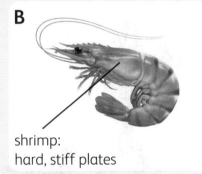
shrimp:
hard, stiff plates

C
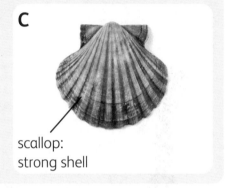
scallop:
strong shell

Classify

6 Name each animal and say whether it has an endoskeleton or an exoskeleton.

A   B   C

D   E   F

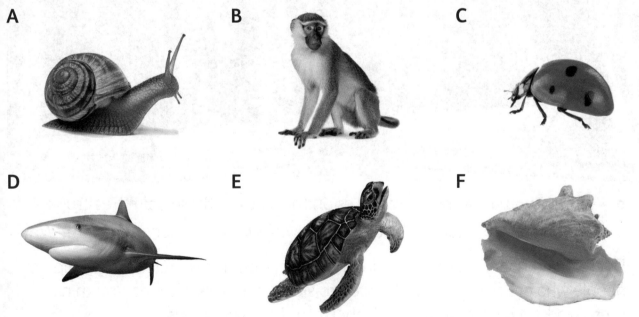

7   Make a list of animals in your environment. Decide whether they have an exoskeleton or an endoskeleton or both.

8   Draw up a table to record the animals you find that have each kind of skeleton.

What did you learn?

1   Look at the picture.

a   Why do you think there are stakes on the sides of these palm tree trunks?

b   Do you think the stakes will be there forever? What will happen to them? Why?

2   Doctors and scientists have developed special robotic exoskeletons to help people who are paralysed or disabled to stand and walk. How do you think these work? Draw a diagram and label it to show your ideas.

Topic 9 Review

Key ideas and concepts

Copy the table. Write or draw a picture in each block to summarise what you learnt in this topic.

Pushing and pulling	Forces at work	Magnets
Making stronger structures	Natural structures	Exoskeletons

Think, talk, write …

A family has decided to build a new home. They need to make sure their home can withstand the force of the wind during hurricanes. Give them some suggestions on how to make their home strong. Think of what they will use to build their home. List some other support structures they can use to ensure the house stays upright.

Quick check

1 Define these terms in your own words:
   a   exoskeleton
   b   structure
   c   magnet
   d   pushing force.

2 List five examples of actions in your daily life that require pushing or pulling forces. Say whether each one is a push or a pull.

3 Look at these two animals.

   a   Which animal has an endoskeleton, and which has an exoskeleton?

   b   What are the similarities between an endoskeleton and exoskeleton?

   c   What are the differences between them?

   d   Plants don't have skeletons. What structures do they have to make them stronger and help them stay upright?

Teaching notes

Prior knowledge

* Students should understand the difference between objects and the materials from which they are made. The materials they should know are wood, rubber, metal and plastic. They should understand that materials have different properties that determine their use.

Physical properties of materials

* Everything around us is made up of matter. Matter is anything that takes up space and has mass: air, our bodies, seawater and rocks are all made of matter. We call the different types of matter that we use for making objects materials.

* Materials have characteristics or properties that affect how they behave. Physical properties are things that can be observed with the five senses, or that can be measured. Size, colour, shape, density, melting and boiling points are all physical properties.

Magnets

* Magnets have specific properties that make them useful in the home and in the community. At home, they can be used to hold things, to keep things closed or to pick up items. They are also used in motors, speakers, bank cards and switches.

Physical changes

* Matter is mainly found in three states: solid, liquid or gas.

* When matter changes state, it undergoes a physical change. This means it changes form, but there are no chemical changes to the substance, and no new substances are formed.

* Many (but not all) physical changes are reversible. When materials are cut or crushed, they change shape, so the change is physical, but not reversible. For example, you cannot get a log back if you chop it into smaller pieces.

A

Look at these containers of food. What are they made of? Could you put these containers into the oven to heat up the food? Give a reason for your answer.

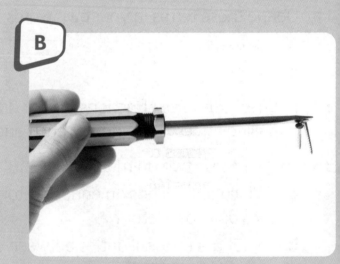

B

This is a magnetic screwdriver. What does that mean? How is this useful for people who use screwdrivers regularly?

C

What is happening in this picture? What will happen when the melted chocolate is taken off the stove? Why?

Think, talk and write

A Physical properties of materials
(pages 142–145)

1 What materials are a good choice for making cooking pans? Share your ideas and give reasons for your choices.

2 Why is it important for engineers to understand how different materials behave when they design and build aeroplanes? List as many reasons as you can.

B Magnets *(pages 146–147)*

Mrs Smith went on holiday and she bought a fridge magnet with a picture on it.

1 How does a fridge magnet work?

2 Will the magnet stick to the kitchen window? Explain why or why not.

3 What else in the kitchen might it stick to?

4 Where are magnets used in your home and community? Work in groups to find as many uses as you can.

C Physical changes *(pages 148–150)*

You already know that water can change from a liquid to a solid, and from a solid to a liquid.

1 When does water change from a liquid to a solid?

2 What makes ice change back to a liquid (water)?

3 What other materials can you think of that can change from a solid to a liquid?

4 Why do water drops form on the outside of a glass of cold juice? (Hint: They don't come from the juice!)

A Physical properties of materials

Science ideas

In this unit you will:

* list some of the physical properties of different materials
* match the properties of different materials and their uses.

Explain

In science we say that everything in the world is made of **matter**. The different types of matter that people use to make objects are called **materials**. Plastic, glass, wood and metal are types of materials.

Materials have **properties** that make them useful for different jobs. Properties that we can observe and measure are called **physical** properties.

Some physical properties of materials are colour, texture, hardness, flexibility, whether the material is magnetic or not, and whether it floats or sinks.

We can test materials to compare and measure their properties. This helps us to decide which materials are best for making different objects.

Key words

matter
materials
properties
physical

Observe and compare

1   Choose three of the objects in the photograph.

   a   Write down what materials were used to make each object.

   b   What properties of each material make it suitable for that object?

   c   Could you make the objects you have chosen from different materials? Share your ideas with your group.

2   Look at a chair in your classroom.

    a What materials is it made of?

    b Is your chair:
*   heavy or light
*   hard or soft
*   smooth or rough
*   brightly coloured or dull?

    c What makes the chair strong enough to sit on?

3   Some chairs are designed to be used indoors or under shelters, others are designed for outdoor use.

    a What properties are important when you design a chair that will be used outdoors? Why?

    b Name two materials that are not suitable for making outdoor chairs. Give a reason why each material is not suitable.

Record

4   Work with a partner.

    a List the materials in the boxes in your book.

metal	rubber	glass	plastic	paper	wood

    b Choose one object made from each material and write its name next to the material used to make it.

    c These words can be used to describe the properties of materials:

> hard   soft   smooth   flexible   firm
> shiny   breakable   stretchy   see-through   light
> heavy   rough   strong   magnetic

Discuss what each word means. Use a dictionary to check the meaning of any words you don't know.

    d Choose the best two words to describe each object you listed. Write these words next to the object.

Materials that work

Infer and communicate

5   This is a cooking pan.

a   Why has wood been used for the handles?

b   Why was a different material used to make the pan?

c   What do you think would happen if the pan was made of plastic and the handles made of metal?

6   Here are three different spoons:

a   What is each spoon made from?

b   Which spoon will heat up quickly if you put it in a cup of hot water?

c   Which spoon will become stained if you put it into red curry?

d   Which spoon will float?

Observe and compare

7 Plastic is a very useful material that can be used to make many different objects. Look at the pictures and read the labels.

A
Holds liquids (waterproof)

Bright colours

Light and easy to clean

Doesn't break if you drop it

B
Easy to clean, doesn't get mouldy

Smooth, so doesn't damage clothes

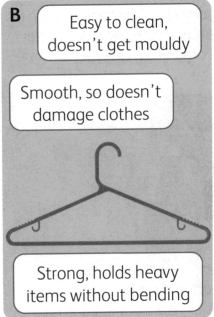

Strong, holds heavy items without bending

C
Doesn't melt in hot water

Floats

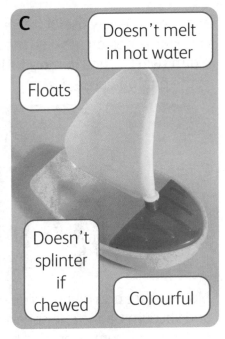

Doesn't splinter if chewed

Colourful

a Find pictures of or draw two metal objects that you use at home. Stick them into your book. Then label them like the pictures above to show why metal is suitable for each object.

b Choose two other objects (not plastic or metal) that you use at home. Find pictures or draw the items in your book. Identify the materials used to make each object. Then label the pictures to show why these materials were chosen.

What did you learn?

1 Write down the most suitable material to make each item.

a Bicycle tyre:	glass	paper	metal	rubber	concrete
b Sun hat:	metal	wood	plastic	paper	fabric
c Sandals:	metal	wood	plastic	foam	rubber
d Serving tray:	leather	glass	paper	metal	fabric
e Mug:	paper	fabric	plastic	metal	glass

2 Write down two properties that make each material you chose suitable for that use.

145

B Magnets

Explain

Magnets are very useful in everyday life. You can find them in cupboard door latches, in the seals of fridge doors, in burglar alarm switches and in **magnetic** organising racks like the one in the photograph.

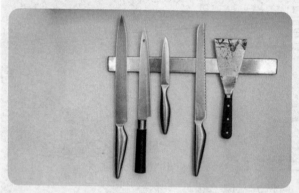

Magnets are also found inside electric motors in hairdryers and vacuum cleaners, in speakers, on the back of bank cards and in many computers and hard drives.

In industry, magnets are used to separate metals from other materials for recycling, to lift scrap metal and to remove tiny pieces of metal from grain and other food.

Science ideas

In this unit you will:
* describe how magnets are used in your home and in the community
* think of other ways to use magnets.

Key words

magnet
magnetic

Observe and compare

1 Magnets can be used to hold things. For example, a fridge magnet can hold papers on a fridge door. List three other ways in which magnets can hold things.

2 Look at these creative ways of using magnets. Discuss how each method works and why it is useful.

A

Magnetic wrist band

B

DIY magnetic pin dish

C

Magnetic sponge

Design and make

The design brief
Work with a partner to design and make something useful that is magnetic.

Step 1: Think and plan
* Decide with your partner what you will make.

Here are some ideas, but you can use your own ideas too:
* a birthday chart for the classroom
* something to keep paper clips together on a desk
* a key holder
* something that stops table cloths blowing away on outdoor tables.

Step 2: Design your object
* Draw your design and label it.
* Make a list of the materials you will need to make it.

Step 3: Make your object
* Gather all the materials you will need.
* Now make your object.

Step 4: Test your object
* Make sure your object does its job well.
* Modify it if necessary.

Step 5: Explain to others how your object works
* Show your completed object to the class and explain how it works.

What did you learn?

1   Look at this handbag.

    a   How can you check whether the clasp is magnetic?

    b   Why do you think it is useful to have a magnet to keep the handbag closed?

2   Work with a partner. Think of ways in which magnets make your life easier. Share your idea with the class.

147

C Physical changes

Explain

All of the matter and different materials in our world can be found in the form of a **solid**, such as wood, a **liquid**, such as water, or a **gas**, such as oxygen. Solids, liquids and gases are known as states of matter.

When you learnt about the water cycle, you saw that water can change **state**. Liquid water changes to a gas (water vapour) when it evaporates. Water vapour changes back to liquid water when it cools and falls as rain.

Science ideas

In this unit you will:

* identify examples of physical changes in everyday life.

Key words

solid	physical
liquid	changes
gas	evaporate
state	melt

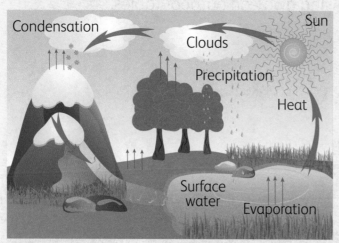

Changes of state are **physical changes**. Physical change means that matter changes form, but doesn't change what it is. So it doesn't change into a new substance. For example, solid ice melts and forms liquid water, and liquid water **evaporates** and forms water vapour.

Water, ice and water vapour are all different forms of water. When solid chocolate **melts**, you get liquid chocolate, but it is still chocolate. If you cool it down, it will turn back into solid chocolate.

Physical changes can also change the shape of a material.

A

Shredded paper is still paper

B

Chopped wood is still wood

C

Crushed stone is still stone

Observe and communicate

1 Look at this ice-lolly.

   a What is happening to the ice-lolly?

   b What is causing the ice-lolly to change?

   c How can you make the ice-lolly solid again?

   d What type of change is this?

2 Your teacher is writing on the board with chalk. She accidentally drops a piece of chalk. When it lands on the floor, it breaks in half. Has the chalk gone through a physical change? Why do you say so?

3 Make a list of different physical changes that happen in your home or community. The changes can involve a change of state or a change of shape. Compare your list with a partner. Check that all the changes you have both listed are physical changes.

Investigate

In this investigation you will observe physical changes.

You will need: 3 small foil dishes, a tea light candle, matches, tongs, a block of chocolate, a blob of butter or margarine, a small piece of candle wax.

Safety note
Be very careful when you work with matches and lit candles.

What you will do:

∗ Put a small amount of chocolate in one of the foil containers.

∗ Hold the container over the tea light candle. Use the tongs to hold it.

* Observe what happens to the chocolate.
* Remove the foil container from the heat (be very careful) and let it cool.
* Observe the chocolate once it has cooled.
* Repeat the experiment with the butter and the candle wax.

Record

* Copy this table and complete it to record your observations.

Substance in the foil dish	Appearance before being heated	Appearance when hot	Appearance when cooled
Chocolate			
Butter			
Candle wax			

Discuss your results

1   What happened to the substances when they were heated?

2   After the substances were cooled, did they look the same as they did before you heated them?

3   How do you know that the changes you observed were physical changes?

What did you learn?

Copy and complete these statements.

1   Some materials melt when they get _____.

2   Some materials turn into solids when they get _____.

3   You can change liquid water back to _____ by putting it into a freezer.

4   You can change ice to water by _____ it.

5   Changes of state are _____ changes.

6   In a physical change, no new _____ are made.

Topic 10 Review

Key ideas and concepts
Give a definition and an example of each term.

1	Matter	2	Materials
3	Physical property	4	Magnetic
5	Solid	6	Liquid
7	Gas	8	Physical change

Think, talk, write …

1   Maria lights a candle. After 30 minutes, she realises that most of the candle wax has melted and turned into a liquid. She blows out the candle. When she comes back later, the candle wax is solid again. Explain what happened.

2   How can a strong magnet be useful at home? Suggest three ways.

Quick check

1   Choose the most suitable material to make each object. Then give a reason for each answer.

Item	Material
An envelope	Rubber, glass, metal, paper
A waterproof coat	Paper, plastic, wood, cloth
A fireguard	Plastic, metal, wood, rubber
A kite	Stone, metal, wood, paper

2   A restaurant in a busy food court finds that lots of metal cutlery is lost because it is accidentally thrown out with the disposable plates and waste food. How could they use a magnetic system to help solve this problem? Draw and label your ideas.

3   a   What happens to chocolate if you leave it in the Sun?
    b   How can you change liquid chocolate back to a solid?
    c   Why is a change of state called a physical change?

Test yourself

Explain

When you write tests, you will be expected to answer multiple-choice questions. There are two types of multiple-choice questions.

Type A – A question with choices for the answer	Type B – An incomplete sentence that you have to finish by selecting the missing piece
1 Which of these materials is not magnetic? 　A Copper 　B Iron 　C Aluminium	2 If you put a glass of cold water on the desk 　A the water will start to boil 　B drops of water will form on the outside of the glass 　C clouds will form in the water

For both types, you need to read carefully and choose the best and most correct answer. Write the number of the multiple-choice question and the letter of the correct answer in your book. For example, for these two questions you would write:

1   C

2   B

Work through the multiple-choice questions on these pages to check that you have understood and can manage the work covered this year.

Your teacher will provide an answer key.

Use the questions you answered incorrectly to plan your revision.

Use this diagram for questions 1 to 3.

1   What does this instrument measure?

A   Thermometer

B   Temperature

C   Wind speed

2   What is the reading shown on the instrument?

A   30 mm

B   30 °C

C   30 °F

3   Where do you think this measurement was taken?

A   In a fridge

B   In a classroom

C   In a cup of hot water

4 When you do a fair test
   A you keep everything the same
   B you change a number of things
   C you change one thing only

5 Which of these are not types of precipitation?
   A Rain   B Hail
   C Clouds

6 Which of these is not a stage in the water cycle?
   A Evaporation
   B Precipitation
   C Innovation

7 Which weather conditions do these symbols show?
   A Sunny and hot with a light breeze
   B Partly cloudy and cool with a light breeze
   C Raining and cool with a light breeze

Monday

21 °C

8 Resources that get used up and that will run out are called
   A rememberable resources
   B renewable resources
   C non-renewable resources

9 What are the main components of soil?
   A Sand, silt and clay

   B Gravel, sand and air
   C Gravel, humus and water

10 Taking in oxygen and using it to produce energy is called
   A photosynthesis
   B respiration
   C atmosphere

11 What force makes it hard to open a car door against the wind?
   A Gravity
   B Air resistance
   C Magnetism

12 Hard water
   A doesn't lather well with soap
   B lathers well with soap
   C is very pure with no minerals

13 Which statement is not true?
   A Earth is the third planet from the Sun.
   B Earth revolves around its own axis.
   C Earth revolves around the Sun.

14 A plant with two seed leaves usually has which of these characteristics?
   A Fibrous roots
   B Leaves with parallel veins
   C Tap roots

15 Which of these is an example of a monocotyledonous plant?
   A Mango   B Bean
   C Rice

153

16 What is it called when strawberry plants grow runners?

  A Sexual reproduction

  B Vegetative reproduction

  C Artificial propagation

17 All of these are conditions necessary for germination except

  A sunlight   B water

  C warmth

18 The process by which a seed turns into a seedling is called

  A pollination

  B germination

  C transpiration

19 To which class of vertebrates does this animal belong?

  A Amphibians

  B Reptiles

  C Snakes

20 Which one of these animals does not have a backbone?

  A Starfish   B Eel

  C Shark

21 Characteristics of invertebrates are

  A backbone, exoskeleton

  B no backbone, exoskeleton

  C backbone, endoskeleton

22 Which of these are mammals?

  A Humans   B Birds

  C Frogs

23 Which animal doesn't belong with the others in this group?

  A Dog   B Turkey

  C Cow

24 Birds that feed on nectar from flowers have beaks that are

  A short and round

  B sharp like a spear

  C long, thin and tube-shaped

Use this diagram to answer questions 25, 26, 27 and 28.

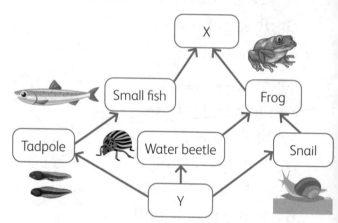

25 What does this diagram represent?

  A The number of organisms living in a habitat

  B The feeding relationships in a habitat

  C The balance of nature in an ecosystem

26 Which of these organisms could replace X in the diagram?

  A Heron   B Seaweed

  C The Sun

27 Which of these organisms could replace Y in the diagram?

   A Heron   **B** Seaweed

   C The Sun

28 Which statement is false?

   A If the plants were removed, the whole food web would collapse.

   B If there isn't enough food for tadpoles, frog numbers will decline.

   C If you remove one organism from the food web it won't affect the balance.

29 Which of these ecosystems are not found in the Caribbean?

   A Mangrove swamps

   B Scrublands

   C Deserts

30 The term *conservation* means

   A protecting and saving natural resources

   B reducing how much waste you throw away

   C different types of pollution

31 _____ is the main source of light and heat on Earth.

   A Oil and gas

   B The Sun

   C Electricity

32 Which of these do not emit light?

   A Stars   **B** The Moon

   C Lightning

33 Which fuel is the odd one out in this group?

   A Charcoal   **B** Petrol

   C Coal

34 Energy stored in coal is transformed into _____ energy when the coal is burned.

   A smoke   **B** heat

   C movement

35 Which of these is a pulling force?

   A Typing on a computer

   B Combing your hair

   C Pressing the on switch on a lamp

36 Which of these statements is false?

   A You cannot see forces.

   B You can feel the effect of a force.

   C Forces cannot change the direction of movement.

37 Which of these items will be attracted to a magnet?

   A Metal paper clip

   B Plastic comb

   C Wooden pencil

38 Which of these materials is likely to be the strongest?

   A Paper   **B** Wood   **C** Iron

39 Which of these processes can strengthen a structure made of paper?

   A Folding it   **B** Wetting it

   C Stretching it

155

40 This view of a tree trunk is called a

   A   slice
   B   cross-section
   C   layer diagram

41 Which of these animals does not have an exoskeleton?
   A   Lobster   B   Spider
   C   Fish

42 Naresh has a material that is light, smooth, shiny and magnetic. Which of these could it be?
   A   Glass   B   Metal
   C   Plastic

43 Wood is used to make the handles of cooking pans because it is
   A   a good insulator
   B   a good conductor
   C   attractive and pleasant to hold

44 Which statement is true?
   A   Magnets cannot be used to hold things because they are not strong enough.
   B   You can find magnets in alarm switches, in hair dryers and in computers.
   C   Magnets are not suitable for use in electric motors because they are made of metal.

45 Changes of state are
   A   permanent changes
   B   physical changes
   C   changes in position

46 Which of these changes cannot be reversed by cooling?
   A   Melting
   B   Evaporation
   C   Freezing

47 Which of these is not a physical change?
   A   Chopping wood
   B   Burning wood
   C   Cutting wood into slices

48 Which process can make an ice block change to liquid water?
   A   Condensation
   B   Melting
   C   Precipitation

49 Marisol wants to make a waterproof cover for her barbeque. Which group of materials could she use?
   A   Rubber, plastic, cloth
   B   Rubber, plastic, paper
   C   Rubber, plastic, metal

50 How do you think you did in this test?
   A   Very well
   B   Reasonably well
   C   Not so well